HIJACK

HIJACK

144 Lives in the Balance

A Firsthand Report

Bunsei Satō

Gateway Publishers Inc.
Los Angeles

Originally published, in 1974, in Japanese, under the title Haijakku (Hijack), by Kodansha (Publishers) Ltd., Tokyo

Distributed in the United States by
Japan Publications Trading Co. (USA) Ltd.
200 Clearbrook Road, Elmsford, New York 10523

Produced and printed in Japan by Kodansha International Ltd. and Dai Nippon Printing Co., Ltd.

LC 75-21530
ISBN 0-914594-03-6

First edition, 1975

Contents

Foreword

I am happy to have been asked to write this foreword, for it gives me a further opportunity to offer my apologies to the passengers of the Japan Air Lines' plane that was hijacked on July 20, 1973, for the great suffering they had to endure. It also gives me the opportunity to express my heartfelt gratitude to the governments and people of Dubai and Libya; to the staffs of British Airways, Gulf Air, Libya Arab Airlines and Lufthansa; and to the staff members of several Japanese trading firms who cooperated wholeheartedly in the rescue of the passengers.

On that July 20, JAL Flight Number 404 was hijacked almost immediately after it took off from Amsterdam's Schiphol Airport. More than three days under the boiling sun of the Arabian Peninsula were to pass before the passengers and crew were again free. Although a JAL plane, the Yodo-go, was hijacked by radical students several years earlier, the Dubai incident was the worst in the history of Japan Air Lines.

The story of that incident is told here by Bunsei Satō, who was at that time the vice minister of transport in charge of parliamentary affairs and who, like myself, was more than willing to become a hostage if in so doing the safety of the passengers and crew could be ensured. In describing what happened in great detail, he also recounts the actions, sometimes heroic and, in the familiar phrase, above and beyond the call of duty, of those whose names have remained unrecorded. This is a human document of the courage of men and women in the face of imminent tragedy.

The mission of an international airline is to provide passengers with safe passage to their countries of destination without regard to nationality, race, religion or philosophy. The greatest and sometimes the most tragic hindrance to the accomplishment of this mission is the hijack. For a single airline or a single country to prevent hijacks from occurring is simply impossible.

International conventions for the suppression of hijacks and sabotage do exist, but there are several countries that still have not ratified them. This is particularly true of Middle Eastern countries, which have their own way of thinking. Thus, we are not at a stage where hijackings can be effectively prevented. Unless every nation cooperates to wipe out this heinous crime from the face of the earth, I fear that hijacks will continue to occur. The alternative under the present circumstances is, I believe, for politicians the world over to concentrate their efforts on the adoption of international and effective countermeasures that prevent hijacks from being attempted.

Nevertheless, politics alone is not sufficient. Strict baggage inspections and body checks are being carried out at all international airports today. As long as the threat remains, these are necessary measures, but, unfortunately, differences of opinion frequently arise between inspectors and passengers over the way inspections are conducted. For those engaged in civil aviation, this is no minor problem. It may be that methods of inspection could be improved, resulting in fewer inconveniences, but at the same time, passengers should be more keenly aware of the threat of hijackings and more willingly cooperative with airline personnel.

I believe that this book appears at an opportune time, a time when people are becoming increasingly aware of the tragedy implicit in the hijacking of aircraft.

In conclusion I would like to relate one episode. While I was at the Bejira Hotel in Benghazi, after the rescue of the passengers and crew, the five non-Japanese passengers came to me and said that "the crew members did a superb job and took good care of the passengers. In a situation that was extremely tense, they remained calm. We would like to shake hands with the president of the airline that employs such a fine crew." It goes without saying that our handshakes were warm-hearted.

In September, 1973, two months after the hijack, two of those passengers, Mr. Gauger and Mr. de Comming, came from the Netherlands to visit Japan and gave a party in Tokyo for the crew, at which I was also present. This was a splendid gesture on their part to show their appreciation for the crew's courage, and I was deeply moved by their sincerity. And it was a further opportunity for me to pay tribute to the crew of JAL 404. In my heart, I felt immense pride in knowing that we had such fine people in our company.

SHIZUO ASADA, PRESIDENT
JAPAN AIR LINES

لقد تجلت الانسانية في عملية اختطاف الطائرة اليابانية عام ٧٣
من جميع النواحي . فكانت ما قمنا به من واجب تجاه سلامة جميع من
كان في الطائرة لذلك قام الطرف الياباني بذلك ولا ننسى
موقف الاخوان الفلسطينيين الذين كانوا على متن الطائرة وموقفهم
وانسانيتهم فانهم كانوا يدافعون عن قضية وان واجبنا تجاه
اخواننا كان يحتم علينا القيام بالعمل بكل حكمة وصبر وبحمد الله
على ان جميع الركاب قد نجوا في هذه بعد ان ضحى الاخوان
الفلسطينيين بحياتهم كانت غالية علينا وعلى جميع العرب في سبيل
نجاة جميع الركاب وهذا دليل واضح على الانسانية الكاملة
والله ولي التوفيق

محمد بن راشد آل مكتوم

I believe that the hijacking of the JAL plane in July, 1973, put my humanism to an extreme test. My actions on that occasion were taken in accordance with my natural duty and my fervent desire to save the lives of everyone aboard the plane. The people who came from Japan to assist in the rescue of the passengers acted with the same desire.

Although my thoughts hovered over the safety of the passengers and crew, I could not overlook the position my Palestinian brothers were placed in. Not only were they fighting for the liberation of Palestine and the recovery of the human rights of its people but they were ready to sacrifice their own lives. Their problems are not theirs alone; they are the problems of all Arab peoples. Thus my natural duty extended to a concern for the protection of the lives of my brothers in the plane.

When I learned that the life of one of my brothers had been sacrificed, I was deeply worried that the others might engage in an act contrary to humanism. Concentrating all our wisdom, my staff and I negotiated patiently. I repeatedly urged those in the plane to act within the bounds of wisdom and patience.

This was my duty toward my brothers. And despite the fact that they had paid a very dear sacrifice, they revealed their humaneness in the release of the passengers and crew. That the incident was solved without death or injury to anyone was the result of the humanism shown by those who came from Japan, my brothers aboard the plane, we ourselves and all others concerned with the incident.

The incident, in which all acted with a feeling and purpose transcending national boundaries, will no doubt leave an indelible imprint in the pages of history. All humanity may be proud of the outcome.

Praise be to Allah Who led us to success!

SHEIKH MUHAMMAD IBN RASHID AL-MAKTOUM
DEFENSE MINISTER
UNITED ARAB EMIRATES

Flight 404

SHORTLY AFTER NOON on a midsummer day, Orly Airport, Paris. The final announcement for Japan Air Lines' Flight 404 came over the public address system. By 12:25 all the passengers were on board, and at 1:00 P.M., on the dot, the Boeing 747–200 lifted off the runway. From Paris to Amsterdam, from there to Anchorage, then on to Tokyo: this is the route that had been followed so many times in the past. None of the fifteen members of the crew and only a handful of the passengers had any reason to suspect that this flight on July 20, 1973, would be any different.

Comfortably seated in the first-class compartment were an attractive, fashionably dressed couple in their middle thirties, who seemed to be newly-weds. The woman was particularly striking, her thick eyebrows, classical features and dark eyes suggesting the typical Arabian beauty. According to their Peruvian passports (later discovered to be counterfeit), they were Mr. and Mrs. Carlos Peralta.

Their seats were 4H and 4J and had been chosen by Mrs. Peralta. At the JAL counter at Orly, the man had wanted to reserve seats in row seven; these are closer to the service bar and the stairs leading to the upper-deck lounge than those in row four, but after some discussion (the language was neither Spanish nor French nor English), he had given in to the woman's choice of row four. The agent at the counter remembered them because of this little incident, without attaching any importance to it.

The hand baggage they presented for inspection at the boarding gate similarly failed to arouse any suspicion; it consisted of a small leather bag, measuring about four by eight by twelve inches, and a plastic bag like those given away at duty-free airport shops around the world. The guard gave them a cursory inspection and asked what they contained.

"Oh, candy and presents for our families," replied the woman.

With a wink, the guard said, "Okay, bon voyage!" (When later informed by the Paris police that the two were hijackers, the guard was starkly incredulous.)

"Mr. and Mrs. Peralta" passed through the gate arm in arm.

Among the fifty-five passengers in the economy-class compartment were three men who had chosen their seats with a single purpose in mind. In the rear was a Japanese youth traveling under the alias A. Miyazawa. It is believed that he was known to his fellow guerrillas as "Asad," but his real name was Osamu Maruoka. Twenty-five years old, he had failed his university entrance examinations and subsequently entered a preparatory school in Tokyo; he soon grew tired of that and from his hometown of Osaka left for a vacation in Europe. There he became involved in the Palestinian guerrilla movement, underwent training in guerrilla warfare, and is suspected of having been involved, albeit not directly, in the massacre of civilians at Lod Airport, Tel Aviv, on May 30, 1972.

In the middle of the compartment was an Arab who went by the name of Akbal and wore a beard. And that is the extent of our knowledge about him even today.

In seat 14C, wearing a red shirt, was another Arab, who called himself "Kassay." At Orly he had asked for seat 11C, directly behind the first-class compartment and next to the aisle, but since rows eleven, twelve and thirteen were being used for baggage, he had had to settle for 14C.

The jumbo jet flew north, toward Amsterdam. It was a comparatively new plane, an improved version of the Boeing 747 with engines redesigned to reduce noise. Purchased by JAL in March of the previous year and registered as JA8109, it had logged 4,405 hours of flight time.

Chief pilot Kenji Konuma had flown aircraft of various types for a considerably longer period of time and was, in fact, one of the most experienced pilots in Japan. Forty-nine years of age, he had begun his career with Dai Nippon Airlines during World War II. As the war intensified, commercial flights were grounded, and Konuma was drafted. He was assigned to fly army transport planes, but before actually doing this, the war ended. He returned to flying commercial passenger planes after the war, and, as of June 30, 1973, his flight time totaled 13,035 hours and 50 minutes, of which 1,919 hours and 58 minutes were spent at the controls of jumbo jets. Now, as he guided Flight 404 over northern France, Belgium and the Netherlands, he had passed the 2000-hour mark. He was, of course, familiar with JAL routes throughout the world, but neither he nor any other JAL pilot was familiar with the skies over the Arabian Peninsula.

The other two men in the cockpit with chief pilot Konuma were Osamu Takagi and Seiji Urano. Takagi, the copilot, had just the previous day celebrated his thirty-ninth birthday. Until two years ago, he had been a pilot in Japan's Air Self-Defense Force; then he had joined Japan Air Lines and seven months previously had passed the examinations that qualified him to be a jumbo jet pilot. At home in Yokohama were his two daughters, waiting for the presents that they knew their father would bring.

Seiji Urano, at thirty-three, had already been with JAL for nearly fifteen years. After graduating from high school, he had qualified as a flight engineer for every type of plane that JAL had flown: DC6, Convair 880, DC8, B747. He had been a flight engineer on the first jumbo jet that the airline had put into service.

There were two other JAL pilots on board, but they were off duty. Seated in the rear of the passenger compartment, near Osamu

Maruoka, were Takeo Saeki and Teiji Kodama, who had flown their plane to Paris and were now returning to Tokyo.

At 3:30 P.M. JAL Flight 404 had completed its routine stop in Amsterdam, and JA8109 sat at the end of the runway at Schiphol Airport, waiting for clearance to take off. The number of passengers had more than doubled; 68 more had come on board, so there were now 130 passengers, all except 9 of whom were Japanese. After a delay of nine minutes, clearance came from the control tower. The weather ahead was reported to be good. "Bon voyage" were the last words from the control tower before the brakes were released and the plane began to pick up speed. Anchorage was eight hours away.

Samil Abdul Mait Ibrahim must have felt a sense of satisfaction, for, at least at this point, things were going according to plan. This was not the first time for him to leave this airport on a similar mission: there had been a previous incident that, like the present one, was marked by violence and ended in fiery destruction.

On September 6, 1970, a woman named Leila Khaled and a man named Patrick Joseph Algero had hijacked an El Al Boeing 707 immediately after take-off from Schiphol Airport. In the gunfight between the hijackers, crew and guards on the plane–it was the only hijack up to that time during which pistols had been fired aboard a plane in flight–one of the guards was seriously injured, and Algero was killed. Although Khaled, who was the leader, was captured, she was later released by the London police in exchange for hostages held by the guerrillas.

While the gunfight was going on, Ibrahim and a man who gave his name as Ali Asaid Ali were waiting to stage another incident. They had planned to be on the El Al flight with Khaled, she in the economy-class compartment, they in the first class. But when the two men had tried to reserve seats, the clerk at the El Al counter had observed that they were shabbily dressed and refused them, saying that all the first-class seats were booked full. Then, for the same reason, he had denied them seats in economy class. They had better luck at the Pan American counter. They boarded a jumbo jet that took off two hours after the El Al flight. Thirty minutes later they hijacked it.

Ibrahim had familiarized himself with the cockpit and instrument panel of the Boeing 707, but as he stood in the cockpit of the Pan American jumbo jet, he found he was unable to read the instruments. Sensing this, the pilot made him believe that they were running low on fuel. They would have to land, but where? From various control towers came the warning that their runways were too short for a jumbo jet to land.

A frustrated Ibrahim finally forced a landing at Cairo airport. He and Ali placed hand grenades at several strategic points in the plane. The grenades, they explained to the passengers and crew, would explode precisely eight minutes after the plane landed. They urged them to get clear as soon as the plane came to a stop. What actually happened shocked the two hijackers as much as it did anyone else. Three minutes after the plane stopped, the grenades went off–five minutes ahead of schedule. Ibrahim and Ali jumped from the plane just in the nick of time and escaped.

Samil Abdul Mait Ibrahim, believed to be known to his cohorts in the guerrilla movement as "Isa," has been identified as the man who now occupied seat 14C under the name of Kassay. About five feet eight inches in height, he was slim, handsome and muscular. Although an Arab born in Jerusalem, he might have been taken for a black on the basis of his dark skin and facial features. His ancestors, it was later learned, had come from Chad.

Eleven minutes had elapsed since take-off. The normal, but not insignificant, hazards of lifting millions of pounds of aircraft, human bodies and cargo from very near sea level to an altitude of thirty-two thousand feet, of accelerating from a standstill to six hundred miles per hour had been passed through safely, as, to be sure, is usual in thousands of flights from hundreds of airports around the world daily. Flight 404 leveled off at cruising altitude; the seat-belt sign went off. It was the moment when crew and passengers alike breathe a sigh of relief. The sky as far as the eye could see was deep blue and absolutely cloudless.

There were now five passengers in the first-class compartment. Two of them, the Peraltas, stood up casually and slowly climbed the stairs to the upper-deck lounge. Just as they had to the agent at the check-in counter at Orly, they seemed to chief purser Nobuhisa Miyashita to be newly-weds. The man took a seat in the back part of the lounge and gazed out the window. The woman also took a seat near a window, but in the middle part of the lounge. Stewardess Hisae Katō, who had followed them up the circular stairs, proceeded to open a bottle and serve them each a glass of champagne. She then returned to the first-class compartment, and chief purser Miyashita went up to the lounge.

The woman's seat was, of course, adjustable, but she did not seem to know how to operate it. Miyashita approached her, crouched down, and showed her how to adjust the seat. "Thank you," she said in English. Soon she had the seat in a reclining position and was swinging slowly from left to right and back again. She seemed to be enjoying this.

Eighty-two hours of terrorism began with a sharp, metallic click. Miyashita remembers hearing it, but he was unable to determine its source because the explosion that immediately followed sent him sprawling on the floor of the lounge. There was also, he remembers, another sharp sound, that of a pistol shot, and perhaps a second pistol shot, but he is not sure about the latter. He lost consciousness momentarily, but before he did, he saw that Mrs. Peralta was no longer in the reclining seat.

"I recall it distinctly," he said. "It was like a slow-motion movie. The woman was flung up from her seat, but slowly, and came down heavily, but still slowly, near my legs."

It was Carlos Peralta who had fired his pistol, but probably inadvertently, having been taken off guard by the explosion. However, he lost no time in descending the stairs. He burst into the economy-class compartment, where Kassay was already on his feet. After a few words were exchanged in Arabic, Kassay's features contorted, as if he were in pain. From his pocket, he tried to pull something out, perhaps a gun, but his hands trembled and he gave up the attempt. Suddenly he yelled, "Jalla, jalla [let's go, let's go]," and rushed into the first-class compartment. He ran all the way to the front before turning around and clambering up the stairs to the lounge.

Chief purser Miyashita's injuries were not insignificant: his right eardrum was broken, as were two teeth in his right jaw; something was lodged in his right eye, and his right shoulder was cut and bleeding, but his vision had cleared enough that he could see what had happened to the lounge. It was a shambles. Through the smoke that still lingered, he could make out dark spots on the walls and ceiling–the blood of the woman, and perhaps his own. Pieces of flesh were scattered here and there.

"The legs of the table," he later reported, "were all broken to pieces, and the top of the table was nowhere to be seen. But the most tragic sight was that of the woman. She was in a sitting position, slumped forward with both legs sprawled out–her head between them, almost touching the floor. It was an unnatural position; there was no movement in her body."

The woman who had so impressed others by her elegance died instantaneously, by disembowlment. The explosion was certainly not part of the plan. Whether Mrs. Peralta anticipated it and used her body to shield its force is not known with certainty. As it was, her body and the top of the table absorbed the major impact, and damage to the fuselage was slight. The outer panes of the double-pane windows were still intact, and only three of the inner panes were cracked. Thus, intentionally or accidentally, her action saved the lives of 144 people.

Kassay entered the lounge and came to a halt in front of Miyashita. He had his gun out. He pointed it at the chief purser and shouted, "If you move, I'll kill you!" Then, glaring, he turned on his heels and headed for the door connecting the lounge with the cockpit.

The time was 3:55, only five minutes after the plane had leveled off from its take-off climb. Although the sound of the explosion had been audible in the cockpit, it had been faint, and the reverberation had been slight. None of the plane's vital systems had been affected; it was still on course. Nevertheless, flight engineer Urano decided to investigate. He stood up and put his hand on the door handle.

Kassay, with Peralta right behind him, charged into the cockpit. A gun in his right hand, a grenade in his left, he shouted, "Hijack!" Copilot Takagi stared at the grenade. From his training in the Air Self-Defense Force, he knew that the safety pin had been pulled and the grenade was armed.

Over his shoulder, chief pilot Konuma took a quick look at Peralta, whose tattered clothes and smoke-grimed face told him that whatever had happened in the passenger compartment had been serious.

The two men, their eyes shining brightly, appeared to the crew to be like soldiers. They ordered the crew to raise their hands and place them behind their heads. Konuma switched the plane to instrument flight and complied. (In Tokyo, it was 11:55 P.M. I was at home, that is, in the apartment allocated to me as a member of the House of Representatives, and I had already retired for the night.

The night air was hot and muggy, and though I do not remember the content, I recall having had a bad dream.)

The hijack signal was picked up at 4:01.

Air traffic control in Amsterdam contacted copilot Takagi and confirmed that the flight was JAL 404. The signal emitted by the plane was also caught in London and Paris, and JAL offices in all three cities informed the head office in Tokyo via telex. Other aircraft picked up the signal and relayed it to ground stations. Within minutes, the electrifying news had spread throughout the world.

The plane was no longer headed north. On radar screens, it could be seen that it had made a U-turn and was now headed south.

At 4:08, Kassay made the following announcement to ground stations: "We are in complete control of the JAL plane. From now on the chief pilot is Al Kassay. The call sign is Mount Carmel. We will answer to no other call sign."

This message was repeated three times.

Shigeharu Hayashi learned of the situation from his wife. When the seat-belt sign had gone off, he had left his own seat and taken one next to the window. Now, he thought, would be a good time to get the task of filling out his customs declaration out of the way. While he was engrossed in this, his wife, Teruko, came over to his seat. There was an anxious look in her eyes as she leaned over and whispered in his ear, "Hijack! Hijack!" She raised her hands up high; he did the same.

Hayashi was sixty-seven and his wife, fifty-eight. He was semi-retired, having been appointed as an adviser to the Tokai Electric Industry Company, and it was the first opportunity that the Hayashis had had to enjoy a trip abroad.

There were many passengers like the Hayashis aboard. Hatsuo

Sakuma, sixty-five, and his wife Masako, fifty-six, had taken a trip to Europe to "see the world while we are still healthy." Mr. and Mrs. Mamoru Kojima, both in their middle fifties, were on their second honeymoon, as were Yoshinao and Kanako Nakamura, aged sixty-one and fifty-nine. Mr. and Mrs. Yoshio Takizawa (aged sixty and fifty-two) had lost their only son in a traffic accident. They thought a trip to Europe would help them recover from their shock and grief. Shigeo Saitō, seventy-one, and his wife, Toku, sixty-nine, were from Tokyo and had not even planned originally to go to Europe. They had first decided to take a trip to the southern island of Kyushu but had then changed their minds. At seventy-five, Mrs. Fusae Aramaki was the oldest passenger; she was accompanied by her thirty-eight-year-old daughter, Miyoko.

Of course, not all of the passengers were sightseers. Akira Shōda, a cousin of Crown Princess Michiko and a professor at Keio University, had been in West Germany to study the situation in that country following the revision of the antimonopoly law. And Dr. Shin'ichi Imura (the only doctor on board) had been studying at the University of Munich, where his wife and daughter, Naoko, had joined him after the completion of his studies. Naoko was four years old, the youngest person on the plane.

While Kassay was radioing his message to the ground, the Japanese hijacker, Maruoka, alias A. Miyazawa, was addressing the passengers. His beret was much too large, making him look a little ridiculous, but he had a gun in his hand and he was shouting in a style more suitable to a street demonstration: "We are not robbers. We are the Sons of Occupied Territories. We have completely occupied this plane. Therefore, all orders will be issued by us. You will obey our orders. Those who do not obey will be severely punished."

Shigeharu Hayashi listened to this and whispered to his wife, "I don't think under the circumstances we'll be able to get back to

Japan on schedule. We'll probably be two or three days late." At this point, neither Hayashi nor any of the other passengers or crew could have any idea of the ordeal in store for them. Some of the passengers even seemed relieved that one of the hijackers was Japanese, but there was no basis for optimism. Both Maruoka and the bearded Akbal were going about their business with efficiency. They had their orders, and it was evident that they had planned carefully.

Akbal, pistol in one hand, hand grenade in the other, escorted passengers from the front rows to the middle or rear of the compartment and pointed out the seats they were to occupy. Family members were separated ruthlessly. Anyone who seemed disinclined to obey orders was threatened with a hand grenade. One woman, for reasons not clear, was struck with the hand grenade and started weeping. However, most passengers obeyed without a murmur. Men were ordered into window seats; women, into aisle seats, an arrangement intended to prevent attacks from the men and make the aisles safe for the terrorists.

Little Naoko and her parents were the only exception. They were allowed to sit side by side in the same row. Grasping a large panda doll in her arms, Naoko looked around her, wondering what was going on. Dr. Imura soon left his seat to treat chief purser Miyashita and offer what aid he could to passengers who were not feeling well. Miyashita's condition, the doctor realized, was serious if not critical. At the very least, he should be hospitalized.

"Hands up!" the hijackers shouted, forcing the passengers to put their hands behind their heads. Even when they tired, they were not allowed to lower their hands. But again an exception was made for Naoko. She would imitate the other passengers, but when she tired and her hands came down, the hijackers said nothing. They smiled, even joked with her. Knowing that their guns and grenades would be useless against her, they treated her gently.

The following orders were given:

"1. Don't move.

"2. Obtain permission before going to the toilet.

"3. Don't talk.

"4. Pull down the window shades.

"5. Hand over all cigarettes in your possession. From now on they will be rationed.

"6. Hand over all cameras, transistor radios, tape recorders and knives in your possession.

"7. Hand over your passports.

"You will not be harmed if you follow our orders."

While the cigarettes were being collected, one man quickly slipped a carton of Kents under his seat, but the passengers who saw this said nothing. In fact, they gave him a wink of approval.

The hijackers then brought each passenger to the front of the compartment and carried out a thorough physical search.

At 4:50 P.M., Kassay addressed a speech to ground stations. This was recorded by the Zurich police.

"We have risen," he said, "to fight for all the people of all countries that have been occupied by the believers of Zionism. We are fighting against Japanese imperialism, which is the handmaid of American imperialism and is manufacturing a great quantity of napalm bombs."

Thus it appeared that the hijackers were members of an organization of Palestinian guerrillas, but hours would become days before Kassay would reveal the name of his group. This was the first time that guerrillas overseas had taken direct action against Japan.

Still flying at an altitude of thirty-two thousand feet, the plane was now on a southeasterly course. When Naoko became tired and started to whimper, one of the hijackers tried to comfort her by making funny faces, but it was in vain. He then took some candy out of his pocket and offered it to her.

At 5:47 the plane passed over Bolzano in northern Italy. As soon as it had entered Italian airspace, three interceptors of the Italian Air Force had taken off to meet it and were now accompanying it. Although the conversation between the fighter pilots could be clearly heard in the cockpit of the JAL plane, Kassay seemed unperturbed.

At 6:24 the plane was over Brindisi, Italy . . . 6:36, over the island of Corfu . . . 7:00, Athens . . . 7:32, over the island of Rhodes . . . no change in altitude.

At 8:00 P.M. the plane entered Lebanese airspace and seven minutes later was over Beirut. Kassay was excited. Chief pilot Konuma could see how agitated he was; even the hand in which he held his pistol was trembling like a leaf.

"Keep good watch," Kassay ordered. "Do you see any aircraft? Israeli interceptors may attack us. But no matter what happens, fly straight on without changing course or altitude."

Israeli fighters had indeed scrambled when the JAL plane approached the skies over Lebanon. The Israeli government was reacting even more strongly than it had when the El Al flight was hijacked by Leila Khaled in 1970. And since then, on February 21, 1973, the Israelis had shot down a Libyan airliner with 113 persons aboard, after the pilot had inadvertently strayed over Israeli-occupied territory while attempting to land at Cairo airport. But the incident that lay behind the present strong reaction must have been the horrendous massacre at Lod Airport only fourteen months previously.

Using automatic weapons and hand grenades, the three guerrillas had opened fire in the airport terminal, randomly killed twenty-eight civilians, including women and children, and wounded an additional seventy-eight persons. The three (two of whom were killed and the third captured) were all Japanese youths affiliated with Palestinian guerrillas. It could only be described as a *kamikaze* attack:

the attackers did not give so much as a passing thought to whether or not they themselves would survive.

Affiliated with the Palestinian guerrillas are youths of many nationalities, and many more are trying to become associated with them or are receiving military training in guerrilla camps. At the time of the Lod Airport incident, however, it was only Japanese youths who had carried out such a brutal attack on innocent civilians. The wanton nature of the attack had plunged the Israelis into the depths of horror and a frenzy of anger.

Although it regarded the terrorists as common criminals, the government of Japan sent an envoy to the prime minister of Israel to offer apologies and gave solatia to the families of the victims. The amount paid was 3.9 billion yen, a sum that, it will be seen, seems to be significant in the present instance.

Among members of guerrilla organizations receiving military training, Israeli intelligence had reason to believe that at least thirty were Japanese. To those who were already engaged in organizing countermeasures, the composition of the hijack team was as yet unknown, but Kassay had radioed that they were resisting Zionism and Japanese imperialism, i.e., their targets were Israel and Japan. It was quite conceivable that another Japanese *kamikaze* youth was among the members of the team.

Fearing a crash landing in a densely populated area, the Israeli government, in addition to closing Lod Airport, took all precautionary measures to preclude an invasion of its airspace. In the town of Herzliyya, ten miles north of Tel Aviv, troops hurrying to Hawk missile sites created an atmosphere of tension among both residents and tourists. At Lod Airport, Japanese chargé d'affaires Atsushi Matsufuji and research officer Noaki Maruyama waited in the office of the vice superintendent. Israeli Minister of Transport Shimon Peres had called Matsufuji and requested that he go to the airport in case there was an opportunity to negotiate with the hijackers.

At 8:15 the JAL plane was over Damascus.

The Arab countries were showing no willingness to receive the hijackers. In Iraq, Kuwait and Saudi Arabia, airports were put on full alert, just as they had been in Lebanon. To discourage communications from the hijacked plane, all airports extinguished their landing lights; officials were hoping and waiting for the plane to disappear. Some airports even took the initiative by radioing to Kassay first. From Beirut had come the message that the airport was full to capacity with large civilian aircraft, so there was no room for the JAL plane to land. Basra airport advised Kassay that "our runways are too short. It would be too risky for your plane to land here." Bahrain announced simply, "We are closed down for the day."

As Arabs, the airport officials were sympathetic to the people of Palestine, whose lands they considered to have been confiscated by Israel. They were ready to offer spiritual support, and though not antagonistic toward Kassay or the Palestinian guerrillas, they were reluctant to become involved in an unpleasant situation by accepting the hijacked plane. Their feelings reflected delicate differences in opinion between the various Arab countries in regard to the Palestine problem.

In Israel and other countries, the messages from the airports were being monitored, and the wire services reported that the JAL plane, having been refused permission to land, was flying about aimlessly. Had the reports been true, Kassay, was, for at least the second time, being very unlucky.

Actually it would seem that, this time, things were going according to plan. Konuma later reported that Kassay "had already decided at the beginning where to land the plane. He had no intention of attacking Israel."

With no concern for the fear and apprehension he was creating on the ground, Kassay flew on nonchalantly, until, just before

10:00 P.M., the plane approached Basra, at the head of the Persian Gulf on the border between Iraq and Iran. He then became very excited and scanned the surrounding skies anxiously. Iran, he explained to Konuma, was, like Israel, their enemy. But there was no sign of any Iranian interceptors taking off; the plane continued in a southwesterly direction along the gulf. In about one hour it reached the entrance to the gulf.

Kassay forced a landing at Dubai Airport. It was 11:10, Amsterdam time. Seven and one half hours had elapsed since the take-off from Schiphol. In Dubai, the time was 2:10 A.M., July 21. In Tokyo, it was 7:10 A.M.

The hijackers repeated their order not to raise the window shades.

Countermeasures

Summer nights in Tokyo are hot and muggy. In the middle of the night and in the middle of a bad dream, my telephone began to ring. I opened my eyes and picked up the receiver.

"This is Yamada of the *Mainichi Shimbun.*"

I had no trouble in identifying my caller. As a reporter for the *Mainichi Shimbun* whose beat was the Ministry of Transport, he used to visit my office at least once every day. On occasion, we had even made a round of bars in the Ginza together.

"Mr. Vice Minister, what are you doing at home at a time like this?" he asked in a voice that was both surprised and somewhat challenging. I had no answer for his question. Why, I wondered, should I not be at home? I looked at my watch. It was 2:39 A.M. I wanted to ask him what he meant by calling me at such an hour. It occurred to me that he might be at a late-hour bar in Roppongi and feeling pretty good. Had he decided on the spur of the moment to ask me to join him? "Never happen," I thought.

I could not quite hide my anger at being awakened so unexpectedly as I asked him, "Well, what do you want with me?"

"Mr. Vice Minister, don't you know that a JAL plane has been hijacked?" he asked.

At these words, I was fully awake. I realized that at this hour of the day the hijack must have occurred overseas, and from Yamada's words I got the impression that it had occurred some time ago. To myself I thought, "At last it's happened. But what is the ministry doing? Why didn't they inform me?"

Each ministry in the Japanese government has two vice ministers; one is the permanent vice minister, and the other is the vice minister in charge of parliamentary affairs. Both ministers and vice ministers can be, and frequently are, appointed from among the members of the House of Councillors or the House of Representatives, in which case they hold two posts, one elective and the other appointive, simultaneously.

The expression that "a parliamentary vice minister is only an appendix" came to my mind then. The *appendix* referred to is the functionless human appendix. Although my predecessors, as well as myself, had endeavored to make the post of vice minister in charge of parliamentary affairs a meaningful one, we had not, it seems been very successful. Why was it that a newspaper reporter knew about the hijack while I was left in the dark? If I admitted this to Yamada, he would probably make some remark about "an appendix."

Shocked as I was, I tried to remain calm. "Do you have any more detailed information?" I asked.

"No, nothing at all," was the reply. "The foreign wire services are reporting that the plane is still flying in a southerly direction. The deadline for our last edition is approaching, and we're short of information. Considering the time of the hijacking, the plane is probably over Turkey by now. I doubt that we'll have more news unless it lands somewhere."

"If the plane lands," I said, "the Ministry of Foreign Affairs will have more information, and they'll inform us. I'm going to my office. You can find me either there or in the office of the director of the Civil Aviation Bureau. Thanks for calling. See you at the ministry." With that I hung up and called for a car to pick me up. My sleeping gown was soaked with perspiration, not all of it caused by the humidity.

As we sped through the streets of central Tokyo, I thought of offering myself as a hostage. There was a precedent for this. In

March, 1971, Japanese radicals hijacked a JAL plane, the Yodo-go. Shinjirō Yamamura, who is a member of the House of Representatives and was then the parliamentary vice minister of transport, offered himself as a hostage and secured the release of the crew and passengers. After accompanying the hijackers to Pyongyang, North Korea, he and the relief crew brought the Yodo-go back to Japan. If worse came to worse, I would follow suit and become the second member of the Diet to offer himself as a hostage. But when and in what way could I make such a move? Since I knew nothing of what was happening to the plane and its passengers, I could hardly formulate a plan. What was more certain was that I was angry at having been kept in the dark.

We arrived at the ministry at 3 A.M., when the plane was over Athens. The front entrance and the offices of the Civil Aviation Bureau were brightly lit, for when nightshift personnel had received word of the incident from JAL's head office, they had called out, in the middle of the night, all of the bureau's male staff members.

When I entered his office, the director, Nobuyuki Uchimura, and four other officials were huddled over a map. He turned to me and said by way of greeting, "Mr. Vice Minister, how good of you to come."

"How good of me to come? What's happened anyway? The first news I received came from Naohiro Yamada of the *Mainichi.*"

Uchimura said calmly, "You must be mistaken. Surely someone informed you first of all."

One of the other officials then began inquiring among his subordinates as to who had notified me, but it turned out that no one had.

"Well, am I right or wrong?" I exclaimed, but it was no time to argue. Something had to be done immediately if the passengers were to be rescued.

"Let's forget about it," I said. "Have you informed the minister and the permanent vice minister?" One of the officials assured me that they had been informed, but still, I thought to myself, even to bureaucrats a parliamentary vice minister is after all only an appendix.

In the late afternoon of July 20, Yūsuke Fukada was in his office, talking on the telephone. Fukada was the director of publicity for JAL's European region and also chief of the public information section. The publicity director of another airline had just asked Fukada if he would like to get together for a drink after work. While he was trying to make up his mind whether to do that or go directly home for dinner, a member of his staff came to his desk and placed a memo on it: "JAL 404–20 hijacked over AMS." Fukada hung up abruptly. It was not long before his office was filled with newspaper reporters, both British and Japanese. Three exhausting days were to pass before he returned home.

JAL's European regional headquarters, which occupy four floors of a building in Great Marlborough Street, London, soon became a beehive of activity. Emergency headquarters were set up in the third-floor office of manager Katsuya Nohara.

Nohara, however, was in Tokyo for consultations with the head office. In his room in the Imperial Hotel, he was awakened by the telephone and informed of the hijack. He dressed quickly and left his room, not to return, for he was to be aboard the first relief plane that left Tokyo.

At the operations center at Tokyo International Airport, JAL established a countermeasures headquarters at 1:19 A.M. (4:19 P.M., July 20 in Europe), within half an hour after the hijack occurred. From Tokyo, JAL ordered all its stations in Europe to have enough staff on duty to keep a close watch on the movements of all JAL planes. Flight 461, which left Tokyo on July 20 for London, was ordered discontinued at Rome so the aircraft would be available for use as a relief plane (passengers were transferred to another airline).

The voice of Kassay, as he made contact with ground stations, was relayed from JAL stations in Europe to the countermeasures headquarters. Nevertheless, just like the aviation bureau, JAL's head office was having difficulty in collecting accurate information.

At 4 A.M., as the eastern sky brightened, I opened a meeting with the director and other officials of the Civil Aviation Bureau to deliberate countermeasures to rescue the passengers on JA8109, which was then approaching Beirut.

Because of the many unknowns in the situation, there was only one decision to be made at the meeting, and that was to send a government representative to the airport where the plane finally landed. It was decided that I was to be the representative. Councillor Shigeya Gotō of the aviation bureau was to accompany me.

Some of the officials were against my going, questioning whether is was necessary for the parliamentary vice minister to take on such a mission. They argued that my job was to stay in close consultation with the minister and permanent vice minister to decide on the most appropriate countermeasures. While I could understand this position, as a politician I believed that actions were more important than mere words or even decisions. My strongly held belief was that a real politician is one who translates words into action.

If it were a simple hijack, that is, one without political objectives, the chances for the survival of the passengers and crew would be far better. The hijackers would demand only that the plane be diverted to another destination, such as Cuba, as has often happened in hijackings in the United States. All the pilot would have to do would be to fly to the designated place, and then it would be reasonable to expect that the passengers and crew would be safe.

But in cases where there is political motivation, the demands are complicated. In the present case, the hijackers were making demands not on the pilot but on countries. Hijacks by Palestinian guerrillas are exceedingly complicated. Since the guerrillas have no way of approaching foreign countries through diplomatic channels, they attempt to hijack not only the planes of a particular country, i.e., Israel, but also planes of nations friendly to it, with the objective of disrupting relations between Israel and other countries. In some cases, of course, the specific objective may be to obtain the release of captured Palestinian guerrillas.

The series of incidents that began with Leila Khaled's hijacking of the El Al plane in 1970 developed into pitched battles between King Hussein of Jordon and the guerrillas in his country–and more than that.

The planes of three other airlines (Pan American, as already mentioned, Swissair and Transworld Airlines) were also hijacked that day, and a British Airways (BOAC at that time) plane was hijacked three days later, on September 9. The Swissair, TWA and BOAC planes were all forced to land at Dawson Airport in Ghahana, Jordan. This had been a military airport for the British about thirty years earlier and had been named for Sir Walter Dawson, the commander of the airport. It has only one runway, but that is perhaps the longest in the world. On September 5, guerrillas cleared the runway of stones, which had accumulated because of disuse.

When the planes landed, Jordanian troops approached the airport and confronted the guerrillas, but a battle was avoided when the government of Jordan and the PFLP came to an agreement. Many, however, particularly the military, were dissatisfied and angry that armed guerrillas could move about the country freely. The situation was so bad that the northern part of the country was virtually occupied by the guerrillas and had, de facto, become their territory.

For their part, PFLP leaders hoped to use the planes and the more than three hundred passengers in bargaining for the release of their comrades in foreign jails. They also wanted to stop American aid to Israel. But the PFLP's position was not understood by the guerrillas, who had already renamed Dawson "Revolutionary Airport" and thought they could immediately exchange hostages for jailed comrades. (Leila Khaled, in custody in England, was one of them.)

Bad feelings on both sides began to build up. Not only were the guerrillas dissatisfied with the slow pace of negotiations, but they were face to face with Jordanian soldiers who, like themselves, were Arabs. Armed guerrillas from all over Jordan began to converge on Amman, and this in turn further irritated the army. On September 16, the BOAC plane was blown up. This was meant to be a sign to foreign countries that the guerrillas's demands were to be taken seriously, but since it was done before their very eyes, it exacerbated the anger of the army troops.

On September 16, King Hussein, backed by the army, dissolved the cabinet that had made the agreement with the PFLP and appointed a new one composed of seven generals and five field grade officers. In a radio address, the king told his people that "the new cabinet has the duty of reestablishing law and order in the country."

Both sides took this as a virtual declaration of war and clashed at Dawson Airport and at several points in and around Amman. And while the U.S. Ninth Fleet came to the aid of Jordan, the Syrian army moved troops to the border between the two countries. What had started as a civil war was quickly turning into an international conflict; Arab states began to take sides, and the possibility was imminent that they would split into two hostile camps.

President Nasser of Egypt, who had long dreamed of Arab unity, was finally able to negotiate a ceasefire on September 27. Khaled and other captured guerrillas were exchanged for the hostages, but for Nasser it was the end. The following day, he succumbed to a heart attack.

The PFLP, though it had lost a great number of soldiers, felt that it had succeeded in its international approach, and since then guerrillas have watched for chances to carry out other hijacks, passengers and crew being a potent tool for them in making demands on countries that they consider their enemies.

Yet no matter how high their ideals, the Palestinian guerrillas violate an important humanistic concept by using innocent citizens as pawns to achieve their political aims. And no matter how kindly they may treat their hostages, their action is basically a mistake from the beginning. Moreover, there is always the possibility that they may change their minds and resort to brutal actions. It is obvious, then, that the passengers and crew of a hijacked plane are in a very precarious position.

For a politician, it is a matter of duty to save the passengers and crew. Although important questions regarding the means of rescue may be decided far from the actual scene, I believe it is the duty of a fighting politician to be where the plane is and to negotiate directly with the hijackers. If necessary, I was determined to board the plane and talk with the hijackers. I was, therefore, in a frame of mind to fly directly to the airport, wherever it might turn out to be, and take charge of negotiations. I was convinced that it would be sufficient if the minister of transport and the permanent vice minister remained at the countermeasures headquarters established within the ministry.

The runway at the end of which JA8109 came to a stop is 12,464 feet long, running from east to west. It is the only runway, but Dubai Airport is equipped with such facilities as ILS and VOR and, though small, meets the minimum requirements of a modern airport. Slightly to the west of the middle of the runway is the control tower, to the right of that is the passenger terminal, and to the left is the cargo terminal.

Aboard the plane, an evening meal, consisting of roast chicken, salad, bread and tea, was distributed to the hostages. Although the passengers had eaten nothing during the seven and one half hours since they left Amsterdam, a great number of them did not touch the food. Others, like Shigeharu Hayashi, seemed resigned to a long period of confinement and forced themselves to eat.

The hijackers were busily stacking grenades around the doors. If attacked by troops or police, they planned to set off the grenades. The passengers were astonished at the great number produced from bags that must also have contained the candy brought aboard. There was enough of the latter for three hundred people, and the hijackers began to distribute it in what seems to have been an effort to allay anxiety.

Naoko was fast asleep. Although only a child, she had no doubt felt the tension. One of the hijackers walked through the aisle, stopped by her side and placed a piece of candy on her lap.

On orders of Defense Minister Sheikh Muhammad ibn Rashid Al-Maktoum, who thought the location of the plane was not favorable for either removing the passengers or attacking it, the control tower requested the hijackers to move the plane.

From the control tower: "This is the control tower calling. JA8109 captain, JA8109 captain, please reply."

In the cockpit, Kassay was gripping the radio microphone. "I'm Kassay, the captain of this plane. This plane is under our command. We are Al Fatah guerrillas. I'm captain of this plane. The call sign is Mount Carmel. From now on, we won't reply to any but this call sign."

"Okay."

"Tower, what do you want?"

"We want to speak to you about various things. Won't you come nearer? We'll allow your plane ample space at a nearer location."

"That's fine. Will you guide us?"

"Yes, of course."

Under the guidance of the control tower, the JAL plane began to move slowly to a parking area in front of the cargo terminal. When it came to a stop, searchlights were directed at it, but they were soon turned off because of strong complaints from Kassay. In the shadow of the terminal building crouched armed police; in ten jeeps were soldiers armed with machine guns, ready to attack on a moment's notice.

"Carmel, this is tower. Can you hear us?"

"This is Carmel. Yes, we can hear you well."

"Is everything all right with the passengers and crew?"

"All passengers are safe. They are calm. One of our comrades is dead. The chief purser has been injured. To me, the injury does not seem serious, but the doctor on board says that he must be taken to a hospital if his life is to be saved. I would like to believe him."

"Good. Release him from the plane immediately. We'll take him to a hospital for treatment. Wouldn't you like us to take charge of your dead comrade's body for a while?"

"Can you promise that you will return the two to us when we find it necessary?"

"Yes, we promise. Could you also release the doctor who treated the chief purser?"

"That's out of the question. We need him here. Let another doctor treat the chief purser."

"Okay."

"We'll accept your kindness. We're grateful to you. Bring a car for the two. There are to be no police or soldiers in the car. No one in the car is to carry arms. We will allow no activities except those necessary to transport the two. This is an order. If you violate it, we'll blow up the plane immediately. This is not just a threat."

"I see. We'll send a car. Open the door of the plane."

"All right. You can use searchlights to light the area, but don't focus them directly on the plane. Be sure to keep the area around the plane well lit."

Chief purser Miyashita and the body of the woman who had been killed were taken to a hospital in the city of Dubai. Miyashita's injuries were not so serious that his life was in danger, but Dr. Imura had succeeded in obtaining his release by purposely exaggerating.

At the hospital, after it had been cleaned and the gaping hole in her abdomen sewn up, the woman's body was preserved by being placed in dry ice. Her handsome face was even given some light make-up.

JAL's head office had been making plans for the relief and rescue of the hostages since receiving news of the hijack. Detailed lists of relief goods were drawn up, and it was decided that the main meals would be prepared in Bangkok.

Food to be prepared included both Western style and Japanese food, the latter not only because nearly all the passengers were Japanese but also because JAL wanted to give encouragement by indicating that a relief team from Japan was near at hand. Drinks and fruits–mineral water, Coca-cola, fruit juices; bananas, oranges, apples–were loaded aboard the relief plane, along with several kinds of canned foods. Clothing for both men and women included underwear, shirts, blouses and stockings, as well as hats and towels, so that passengers would be able to change clothes on the plane. Travel kits included medicine and vitamin pills among their contents. There were also presents to be given to those who assisted in the rescue: watches, transistor radios, cigarette lighters, Japanese dolls, *happi* coats and ball pens. (When they saw the list of relief goods, employees of Pan American were astonished and exclaimed, "What wonderful service!")

The relief plane waiting at Tokyo International Airport was a DC8 (JA8017). Detailed aerial maps of those districts over which JAL pilots had not flown were collected. JAL President Shizuo Asada was scheduled to board the relief plane with twenty-seven members of his staff, including Director Tonao Senda, Katsuya Nohara, manager of the European region, and Yoshiyasu Mayumi, chief of the secretarial section.

Asada intended to offer himself as a hostage as soon as he arrived at his destination. If the hijackers agreed, he planned to board the plane with twenty-two staff members as soon as all the passengers were safely off the plane. They would then stay on the plane until they were all rescued. He was even hoping that the ten stewardesses would be allowed to disembark. They were, after all, only young girls (their average age was twenty), who at home would be very much their parents' daughters. He could imagine that they were putting up a brave front, comforting the passengers with cheery smiles, while trying to assuage the excitable feelings of the terrorists. But even for them, he thought, rescue operations should be hurried.

The only person to whom Asada revealed his intention was Mayumi. One reason was that he did not want to cause any further agitation by announcing his intention. He also knew that his staff would be violently against his plan, and the rescue plan itself might fail. There were some who were against his making the trip in the first place. Even Mayumi said, "I don't think it is a good idea for you to go personally. Why don't you send someone in your place? I believe that if you take over after the rescue has been completed, it won't be too late."

Asada, however, thought differently, saying, "The hijackers would put more value on a hostage if he were the president of the airline. The more valuable the hostage, the easier it will be to negotiate and the sooner the rescue operation can be completed." Mayumi had nothing to say when he heard this.

A hijacking is an unreasonable action, outrageous and unlawful, but nothing can be solved merely by attacking the unreasonableness. By offering himself as a hostage, Asada would in effect condone the action of the hijackers, no matter how unlawful or unreasonable it might be. Yet, because the terrorists were in a position to make unilateral demands, Asada felt he had no alternative.

Director Senda had a feeling that the president would offer himself as a hostage. Not liking the idea, he wracked his brains for some way to save both Asada and the passengers at a stroke. The only way, he decided, was to give himself up as a hostage in Asada's place.

Sheikh Maktoum ibn Rashid Al-Maktoum, prime minister of the United Arab Emirates and ruler of the sheikdom of Dubai, conferred with his son, Sheikh Muhammad ibn Rashid Al-Maktoum. Although he was only twenty-three years old, he was the defense minister of the United Arab Emirates. The father said simply, "My son, go and negotiate with the hijackers. I cannot leave this task up to any other person."

The prime minister had great confidence in the ability of his bold, resourceful son, and this confidence was shared by Sheikh Zaid ibn Sultan an-Nahayan, the president of the United Arab Emirates. He said, "Rashid will do a good job." But even if he had not been told to do so by his father and the president, Rashid had already made up his mind to negotiate directly with the hijackers and had moved into action before receiving orders.

It was 5:40 A.M., and the midsummer dawn was breaking on the northeastern horizon when Rashid, a muscular man dressed in the typical Arab burnoose and wearing sandals, entered the one-hundred-foot, cylindrical control tower. He took the two-man elevator up as far as it went, got out and climbed the steep, narrow iron stairs to the control room itself. The only sound coming from the plane was the soft purr of a motor used for air conditioning.

A man in the control tower who had been watching the plane constantly during a sleepless night told Rashid that he had seen a figure moving in the cockpit only a few minutes ago. Rashid settled down and waited patiently for further developments.

At 9 A.M. he made his first call. "This is tower, Mount Carmel. To Mount Carmel from Dubai."

"Yes, this is Carmel," Kassay replied.

"Can you hear me well?"

"Yes, I can. What do you want?" Kassay did not know that the man he was talking to was the defense minister and the son of the prime minister. Whether this was fortunate or unfortunate, I do not know, but when, much later, he was informed of this fact, Kassay was surprised and profoundly impressed and began then to speak in a more polite style of language.

"Do you need anything?" Rashid asked. "If you need anything, please feel free to ask for it."

Kassay, seemingly surprised, replied, "Why are you being so kind to us? Why?"

"I am an Arab. I would like to speak to you in the spirit of the Koran. Are you an Arab?"

"Yes, I am. I'm a Palestinian."

"That's fine. Then I think you will understand my mind."

"I will try. I hope that you, too, will try to understand the mind of the Palestinian." On both sides, the talks began with an attempt to confirm their mutual spiritual standpoints.

"The tragedy of Palestine is also our tragedy."

"Thank you. I'm happy that you understand us."

"But we do not extend a welcome. Please understand that. Even so, since you have landed at an airport of the United Arab Emirates, I promise to exert all my efforts toward securing the safety of the people on the plane. Are the passengers and crew all safe?"

"Yes, they are."

"What are they doing right now?"

"They're all asleep. Everyone is calm."

"Have you caused them any injuries?"

"No. Now let me do some questioning."

"Ask anything you wish."

"Where is the body of our comrade?"

"It's in a room at the hospital. The body of the woman has been thoroughly cleaned by a doctor. Her face has been made up. She looks beautiful, even in death. Rest assured that we will treat the body with great reverence. This is not a lie, because I myself saw the corpse."

"Thank you very much. I'm grateful from the bottom of my heart. She was a very important person to us."

"I sympathize with you. Could you tell me how she died?"

"Ask the chief purser, Miyashita. He's the one who knows all the details of her death. How are Miyashita's injuries? Please return him to us after he has been treated."

"I don't think that will be possible. He's in critical condition. When he arrived at the hospital, he was unconscious, and he hasn't recovered yet."

"It can't be helped then. But please return him to us when he has recovered."

"I promise to do that. Where's the crew?"

"They're in the passenger compartment."

"Is the chief pilot near you?"

"*I'm* the chief pilot. Don't ask such a stupid question again!"

"I'm sorry. I'd like to ask some questions about the condition of the plane. Could you let me talk with the former chief pilot!"

"No. Absolutely not! If you have anything to ask, ask me. I'll do the replying."

"Aren't the passengers hungry?"

"We distributed candy to them as soon as we landed."

"I'm talking about meals, not candy."

"Wait a minute. I want to explain about the candy."

"All right."

"The candy was purchased by our comrade whose body is now with you. She wanted to comfort the passengers. I hope you understand how we feel toward them."

"I'm grateful for that. But what about meals?"

"We distributed flight box lunches. They ate them and went to sleep. No, they aren't hungry."

"Thank you for your humanity. Do you need anything?"

"Not at the present moment. We'll let you know later if there's anything we want."

Seated next to him at Rashid's own request–in fact he had driven him to the airport–was Hideo Kyōno, an employee of the Chūtō ("Middle East") Oil Company and the only Japanese living in Dubai. When the plane landed, Kyōno offered his services, which were gratefully accepted by the Dubai government, since the crew and almost all the passengers were Japanese. (There were now roadblocks on the roads leading to the airport, and it was guarded by troops to prevent allies of the hijackers from infiltrating the area.)

Seeing that the conversation between Rashid and Kassay was at an end, at least for the time being, Kyōno went to the hospital. The information he received from Miyashita and relayed to Tokyo via London was the first news JAL had on the explosion.

There was at this time no means of direct communication between Dubai and Tokyo. A telephone call between the two cities had to be routed through several relay stations, and there was, of course, no way of knowing how long it would take for a call to be connected. Thus Kyōno, though he neither worked for JAL nor represented the Japanese government, was a vital link in communications and remained so until the arrival of the relief team.

A roundabout means of communication had been established through Paddy Flack, the manager of JAL's passenger section at Heathrow Airport. Ordinarily he could be found at the counter advising passengers on various matters, but when he heard that the emergency headquarters in London was looking for a way of communicating with Dubai, he called a friend of his at BOAC. Gulf Air he learned, was a subsidiary of BOAC and had an office in Dubai.

Explaining to his friend that a formal request would be made later from JAL to BOAC, he managed to establish an open line between Dubai and the passenger center at Heathrow. Open lines were also established between Heathrow and the regional headquarters and between the latter and Tokyo. This route was later supplemented by a line from Kyōno's office to Heathrow.

Other airlines and an oil company were not the only ones engaged in bridging the chasm between Japan and Dubai. When Mitsubishi Trading Company's head office learned of the Dubai landing, it ordered Takanori Kitahara, its representative in Abu Dhabi (eighty miles southwest of Dubai) to go to Dubai. Kitahara opened a line between Dubai and Abu Dhabi. From there a line was opened to Mitsubishi's head office, and then, by means of a special switchboard, one was opened with JAL's head office.

Kitahara reported the situation at 4:10 A.M., 5 A.M. and 9:30 A.M. (9:10 A.M., 10 A.M. and 2:30 P.M. in Japan). The last of these reports was as follows: "As of 9:30 A.M. today, the weather is fair with a temperature of 100 degrees and relative humidity of 85 percent. Negotiations with the hijackers are being conducted personally by Defense Minister Rashid. At present. there are no signs of any progress being made on the release of the passengers."

Unknown Demands

News of the Dubai landing reached the Ministry of Transport at 7:45 A.M., thirty-five minutes after it occurred. Since I had taken a special interest in Arab affairs and had made two trips to Arab countries, I considered myself more knowledgeable than other members of the Diet, but I have to confess that I knew nothing about Dubai, nor did I have an inkling of where the country was located.

I was not alone in my lack of knowledge; no one in the Civil Aviation Bureau had ever heard of it. We were even unsuccessful in our attempts to locate the name on a map, but perhaps this was due to our excitement over news of the landing.

Even the information we received from the Ministry of Foreign Affairs was meager. When we contacted them, we learned only that "the United Arab Emirates is composed of seven sheikdoms located at the mouth of the Persian Gulf. It was established in 1971. The sheikdom of Dubai is one of the seven. Japan does not have diplomatic relations with Dubai; consequently there is no Japanese embassy or consulate in that country. Only a few Japanese engineers are stationed in the oil district of Abu Dhabi. There are no Japanese in Dubai." (The last point was in error. As already mentioned, Hideo Kyōno was there.)

"If Dubai is a sheikdom, it must be one of those countries inhabited by Bedouins," someone muttered. "I can't understand how a jumbo jet could have landed in such a desolate place. The pilot must have had a hard time landing." His words were indicative of our meager knowledge at that time, and when I later went to Dubai, I was shocked at our gross misunderstanding.

"Of all places, why did the plane land in such a desolate country?" I thought out loud. I had the feeling that my trip would be fraught with difficulties.

As I returned to my official residence, I thought of the passengers. That the plane had finally landed must have given them a sense of relief. Perhaps they were about to take a much needed nap, but it could not be a peaceful one, since they were being closely watched by their captors. I felt that it was a matter of great urgency that I fly to Dubai and conduct negotiations.

As soon as I reached home, I began preparing for the trip. Usually my wife does my packing, but this time I did it alone, throwing shirts and underwear into a suitcase at random. My wife stared at my feverish activity, her face a mirror of amazement and consternation.

Just then the telephone rang.

"What are you doing? Go quickly!" I was advised. It was Shinjirō Yamamura, who had become a hostage in the Yodo-go incident. We were good friends, having met frequently at Diet sessions, and I was relieved to hear his familiar voice.

"Fly immediately to Dubai, no matter what anyone may say," he continued. "Don't leave it up to the Ministry of Foreign Affairs or the National Police Agency. It will take too much time for them to find a solution. The quickest way is for you, as parliamentary vice minister, to conduct direct negotiations with the hijackers. Go immediately! There may be some opposition, but forget about it. Remember, the passengers are at the mercy of the hijackers. Don't forget that for a moment!"

Coming from Yamamura, I thought this was good advice, although news of arguments against my going had already reached my ears. In fact shortly before dawn, a newspaper reporter had come into my office and said, "Mr. Vice Minister, you're now assured of being reelected, aren't you?"

His expression seemed to me to be servile. I knew what he was trying to say, but I asked, "What am I assured of?"

He seemed to be stuck for words. "Aren't you going to offer yourself as a hostage?"

"That hasn't been decided yet," I retorted.

"What, aren't you going to become a hostage?" he asked as if thunderstruck. For my part, I had no desire to continue this kind of talk.

It goes without saying that elections are an integral part of a politician's life, but the current custom of construing every act of a politician as being connected with elections I find distasteful. Even Yamamura, who did not know what would happen to himself, was accused by some of having acted as he did in the hope of being reelected. Similar accusations were being made against me, but I consider such thinking cynical rather than objective.

Professor Gerald Curtis took a different view. In order to make a detailed analysis of my election campaign, he once spent a whole year living with me and my supporters. His report, which became his doctoral dissertation, was translated and published in Japanese under the title *Daigishi Tanjo* ("Birth of a Member of the Diet"). He is now director of the Institute of Far Eastern Studies of Columbia University.

Seeing news of the hijack on television, Professor Curtis called me from New York. He said, "I'm sure you'll give yourself as a hostage. Since there's a precedent, you'll be called a coward if you don't. If you do go, you'll probably be accused of being motivated by hopes of personal gains in the coming elections, because that's very common in Japan. But don't worry about the accusations. Do what you believe should be done!" I was very happy to hear such encouraging words.

I returned to the ministry and at 9 A.M. attended a countermeasures conference presided over by Minister of Transport Torasaburō Shintani. He took a cautious attitude toward my leaving for Dubai immediately, saying, "It won't be too late for you to go after the government has studied the demands of the hijackers, which they are sure to make."

I said, "Do you think the incident should be left entirely up to JAL and government officials far removed from the scene? My opinion is that the problem could be solved more quickly and amicably by my going and negotiating directly."

"A parliamentary vice minister is not a soldier in the front lines of battle," the minister replied. "True, he must sometimes make decisions wholly on his own without consulting anyone, but before you leave, I want you to attend the conferences and firmly grasp the policies of the government. It would be quite inconvenient to have to consult with the government on every action you propose to take in Dubai." This seemed quite logical to me and I had nothing to say. He continued, "I plan to compile a list of hypothetical demands and their answers. I'd like you to put off your departure until after this has been done."

The figure of Minister Shintani loomed large before my eyes, and I realized that in my eagerness for a solution I was perhaps being too hasty.

No conclusions were reached at the meeting, due to the lack of information from Dubai. Although it had been two hours since the landing, no demands had been made. This in itself was out of the ordinary, a situation not seen in any previous hijack perpetrated by Palestinian guerrillas.

In the series of hijackings that began with Leila Khaled, various demands were made, and in the hijacking of a Lufthansa plane in February, 1972, the demand was for ransom money totaling 5 million dollars. But in all previous cases the demands were made almost immediately after the plane landed and then negotiated by other members of the guerrilla organizations who were not involved in the actual hijack. It was only in the present case that neither the hijackers nor, apparently, their organization, which must exist somewhere, were making demands as soon as the plane was on the ground.

Action at the foreign ministry was proceeding at a snail's pace, but I did learn from that source that the government of Dubai was being approached through diplomatic channels for permission to enter the country. It would be some time before approval could be granted.

Not only were there no diplomatic relations–there had never been a single contact between Japan and Dubai–but none of the ambassadors to Arab countries were at their posts. In the middle of July, they had all come to Tokyo for consultation.

During the conference, the ambassadors had been unanimous in their opinion that relations between Israel and the Arab states were not so tense as to lead to another outbreak of open warfare, at least for the time being. They also said that there was little indication that the Arab states would clamp an embargo on oil exports. This was only three months, however, before the Yom Kippur war and the oil embargo by the Organization of Petroleum Exporting Countries, which is suggestive of the difficulty of making accurate appraisals of the volatile situation in the Middle East.

The ambassadors, who following the conference were taking home leave in various parts of Japan, were called back to Tokyo and ordered back to their posts immediately. But bad luck sometimes follows misfortune, and it took a while to locate Ambassador Yoshitaka Ishikawa. He was the ambassador to Kuwait, the Japanese diplomatic post nearest to Dubai (540 miles northwest).

The relief plane, whether permission to enter Dubai had been obtained or not, was to leave at noon, and Ambassador Ishikawa was to be among the government officials on board, if he could be located. As it turned out, he had taken his family to a hotel on the shores of Lake Yamanaka, near Mount Fuji, and being in a relaxed, vacation mood, was paying little attention to newspapers or television or the radio. He was contacted, but not in time for him to reach Tokyo by noon.

Throughout the day, July 21, Defense Minister Rashid was in contact with the hijackers, but his many attempts to obtain concrete information were frustrated.

"From Dubai to Mount Carmel. Can you hear me?"

"This is Carmel. Yes, I can hear you well."

"Isn't it hot in the plane? The temperature must have risen after the sun came up."

"The temperature in the plane is being maintained at 77 degrees."

"That's good. You're more comfortable than we are on the ground. Are the passengers all well?"

"They're all calm."

"Aren't you going to release them? I want you to release them to me."

"I can't do that."

"Why can't you?"

"We're soldiers. We don't have the authority to release them."

"I should like to correct the expression 'release.' It should not be *release* but *liberate*. The term *release* is used when a country, in the name of its people, releases persons who have been captured by the country. You should use the word *liberate*, not *release*."

"I would like to refute your interpretation of the word. It was not through a personal whim that I have taken away the freedom of the passengers. It was through the will of the people of Palestine. We are only servants of that will and have acted accordingly. I think it's only natural that I should use the word *release*."

"I've contacted the PFLP through Beirut. They say they have no connection with your present actions."

"It's necessary for you to realize that there are numerous organizations of the people of Palestine."

"That I know very well. Could you tell me the name of your organization?"

"Wait a minute. I'll answer after we've had time to consider it."

The passengers and crew were fastened tightly in their seats by seat belts, and their hands were held high over their heads. One man, Kazuhiko Matsuo, had counted the number of times they were ordered to hold up their hands and muttered to himself, "This is the tenth time. I wonder how many more times . . ."

At every opportunity, the hijackers screamed, "Hands up! Hands up!" If anyone lowered his hands, he was immediately threatened; sometimes a hand grenade was brandished over his head. Once, they had to hold up their hands continuously for two whole hours.

Naoko mimicked her parents and went through the motions of raising her hands and then lowering them, but she did not laugh, regardless of how much the hijackers tried to humor her. As the passengers gradually became accustomed to their captors, there were some who winked at the terrorists when they passed near them. Among them, however, it was only Naoko who was not afraid.

The conversation between Rashid and Kassay was resumed.

"From Mount Carmel to Dubai."

"This is Dubai. Have you finished your deliberations?"

"Yes, we have. But we cannot give you a reply now."

"That's regretful. Can you tell me the number of your comrades?"

"We can't answer that question."

"Are there any Japanese among your comrades?"

"I told you before that ours is a joint action between a Palestinian people's organization and the Japanese Red Army faction. You can draw your own conclusions."

"I know that. But what I'd like to know is whether there is a Japanese participating in the action."

"What does the Japanese purser say?"

"He's unconscious. He can't speak."

"Is he seriously injured?"

"Yes, the doctor has been with him all night".

"I didn't think his injuries were so serious, but I'll take your word for it."

"Could you give me a reply to my question?"

"Since it's a joint operation, you may assume that there is a Japanese comrade among us. As a commando, he's superior to us. Is this reply satisfactory to you?"

"It's not enough, but I suppose I'll have to be satisfied."

Miyashita had already indicated that the number of hijackers was four or five and that one of them seemed to be Japanese. And, of course, his injuries were not critical. Defense Minister Rashid was continuing the misrepresentation that began with Dr. Imura, suspecting that if the terrorists knew Miyashita's injuries were not too serious, they would intensify their demand for his return. Rashid did not know the doctor, but he had great respect for the courage he had shown in having gotten even one hostage off the plane.

The first relief plane left Tokyo International Airport at 12:19 P.M. No permission for landing had been received at that time from either the United Arab Emirates or Dubai, nor had the hijackers made any demands. (Because I wish to thank them for their efforts and also let the reader know what kind of persons engaged in the relief work, I have given a complete list in figure 1.)

Asada decided that the first stopover would be made in Bangkok and hoped that during the flight further information would be received. It was an uneasy flight, but he wished to get as close to Dubai as possible with the least practicable delay.

Figure 1

THE RELIEF TEAM

From the Government

Shigeya Gotō, Ministry of Transport
Akira Ishizaki, National Police Agency
Toshirō Ogushi, Ministry of Foreign Affairs

From Japan Air Lines

Shizuo Asada, President
Tonao Senda, Director
Katsuya Nohara, European regional office
Sōichirō Kishida, passenger division
Shin'ya Akiba, TIA branch office
Akira Oikawa, airport security section
Kōichi Hiraki, international affairs section
Yasuo Ishibashi, TIA international passenger section
Hideyo Narita, cargo division
Satoru Nakamura, TIA international passenger section
Yoshiyasu Mayumi, secretarial section
Tetsuo Yoneoka, passenger affairs division
Tetsuzō Tsujita, TIA cargo and mail section
Haruo Nakata, TIA cargo and mail section
Kazuo Ogata, TIA international passenger section
Keitetsu Matsuyama, labor relations division
Ototsugu Yamaguchi, physician
Mitsuo Sasaki, physician
Toyoko Ishikawa, nurse
Shigeko Sano, nurse
Hirosuke Yamamoto, Tokyo branch office
Toshikazu Yamaguchi, flight division
Toyoaki Ogawa, information systems division
Muneo Sakurai, TIA management division
Hisamitsu Kunieda, mechanic
Sachiyo Sakurai, mechanic
Kazuyoshi Ōta, mechanic
Tadao Fujimatsu, public information section

Masaru Asama, chief pilot
Satoru Kumagai, chief pilot
Keizō Ishihara, chief pilot
Kōji Kawase, chief pilot
Katsura Matsui, flight engineer
Ikuo Tomita, flight engineer
Kusuo Tanaka, chief purser
Haruki Ōjimi, purser
Sadao Kawano, purser
Masao Minami, assistant purser
Kōichi Makino, assistant purser
Ken'shichi Horiuchi, assistant purser
Yoshinori Fujii, assistant purser
Yasuharu Ozaki, steward
Akiko Yamawaki, stewardess
Keiko Shōjima, stewardess
Mariko Kimura, stewardess
Shigeko Kimura, stewardess
Kimiko Kunitani, stewardess
Yūko Katano, stewardess

From the Media

Mitsuo Miyajima, Kyodo News Service
Ryūjirō Fujita, *Tokyo Shimbun*
Akira Saitō, *Yomiuri Shimbun*
Takashi Kutsuwada, *Asahi Shimbun*
Nobuhisa Ikuhara, *Sankei Shimbun*
Takao Igusa, *Mainichi Shimbun*
Sakujū Maki, *Nikkei Shimbun*
Yoshiaki Numadate, Jiji Press
Kō Taguchi, Nippon Television
Toshio Matsumura, representing commercial broadcasting companies
Naohiro Katō, NHK
Kazuo Ishiwata, Kyodo News Service

TIA—Tokyo International Airport
Shimbun means "newspaper."

At thirty-two thousand feet, the sky was deep blue and without a cloud. Although flying conditions were ideal, the only sound was the steady throbbing of the engines. A good many of the team sat in window seats, lost in deep thought. Yoshiyasu Mayumi paced back and forth between the cockpit and the compartment, anxiously waiting for news from Tokyo.

Asada and his staff sat in the first-class compartment with nine government officials and two physicians. In the economy-class compartment were other JAL employees, journalists and nurses. In the ordinary course of events, as soon as the plane had taken off, someone from Asada's staff would have called on and chatted with the journalists, but no one left the first-class compartment for that purpose. There was nothing to tell the reporters.

One of the government officials was Akira Ishizaki, chief of the National Police Agency's security research section. He had only recently returned to Japan from Paris, where he had been sent on a two-year assignment to serve with the Japanese embassy. He was unique among Japanese law enforcement officers in that he had been a hostage on a hijacked plane.

When the plane was hijacked by a man who wanted to go into exile in Cuba, the chief pilot was not a bit flustered. He called the control tower and said, "There's a passenger aboard who wants to go to Cuba. May I take him there?"

The tower's reply was, "You may go but be careful. Ask the man whether he's willing to pay the extra fare." With that, the plane made a round trip to Cuba, returning intact. But the current case was different. It was not a simple hijacking. Still, if the reporters had gotten wind of Ishizaki's experience, they would without a doubt have pounced on him like so many birds of prey.

Ishizaki was, incidentally, only the second Japanese to be involved in a hijack as a passenger. The first had been Shigeo Yamada, manager of JAL's Tokyo branch office. Ten years earlier, he had been the manager of the branch office in Los Angeles, and in October, 1963, he was aboard an Eastern Airlines flight hijacked by terrorists, who ordered the plane to be flown to Cuba. It was a strange coincidence that the Tokyo branch office was to be involved in the Dubai incident, but neither Yamada nor Ishizaki, nor anyone else for that matter, was yet aware of it.

Ishizaki was still not accustomed to the fact that he, from among all the men in the police agency, had been chosen to go to Dubai. He had heard the news of the hijack in the middle of the night and had remained in his office, collecting information. A little after 9 A.M., he had held a press conference and passed on to reporters the information that he had obtained. The order to go with the relief team came just after that and allowed him only one hour to get to the airport.

At first he thought of calling his wife and asking her to take a change of clothing to the airport. Since there was not enough time for that, he asked one of his subordinates to contact the police agency office at the airport and have them purchase underwear, a safety razor and blades, and a toothbrush and tooth paste and deliver them to the relief plane. Everything was placed in a paper bag, along with some chewing gum that the airport staff was thoughtful enough to include among other items. When Ishizaki received the paper bag on the plane, he suddenly burst out, "I forgot to give them money for these things!"

The relief plane arrived in Bangkok at 5:44 (Japan time). Permission to enter Dubai had not been received. The flight crew settled down to figure out a new schedule.

Whenever Rashid touched on the name of his organization, Kassay's voice took on a hard tone. Rashid had to change the subject.

"Could you tell me your demands?"

"We have no demands."

"Then why are you in Dubai? What's your purpose?"

"We're waiting for instructions from our organization."

"When will the instructions reach you?"

"We don't know."

"I've come to understand your position a little. I'd like to talk with you about this problem at the next opportunity."

"I understand. But I can't say whether I'll be able to satisfy your request."

"Have you had breakfast?"

"No. There are some snacks on the plane, but since they were prepared quite some time ago, we intend to throw them away."

"Let me bring you and the passengers and crew some breakfast. Will you accept?"

"We're grateful for your kindness. Yes, we'll accept."

"What about drinking water?"

"We have only a little left."

"Then we'll bring you some water too."

"You don't have to do that. We know how precious water is in your country. No, we can't accept water."

"I'm terribly moved by your words, but this is my understanding. You, the passengers and crew, as well as we the people of Dubai, are all in Dubai territory right now. Dubai's water is for those who are in Dubai. You and the passengers and crew have a right to the water of Dubai. This is my interpretation."

"I'm extremely moved by your gallant words. We'll accept your proposal with pleasure."

"Thank you. We'll start preparations immediately. Please open the door and wait for us."

"All right. But I'm afraid I'll have to caution you on one other matter. There mustn't be any armed men among those who bring the food and water to us. And you must keep the number of men to the minimum."

"That's understood. I have no intention of creating any disturbance between us right now."

"Thank you."

"Since two persons have left the plane, there are 143 remaining. Is that right?"

"You certainly have a good grasp of the situation. I'm surprised at the extent of your knowledge."

Sandwiches were already being prepared at the Carlton International Hotel in the city of Dubai, and these were soon on their way to the airport on Rashid's orders. When the truck carrying the sandwiches and the truck carrying water were about to move toward the plane from the tower, Kassay suddenly began speaking in a very excited voice.

"A fire engine is coming toward us. What's the reason? What are you planning to do?"

"It has nothing to do with you. It's only a routine we carry out every morning here."

"You're telling the truth, are you?"

"Yes, believe me."

"There's nothing else I can do. I hope you have no other purpose in mind."

"All right. I'll call back the fire engine. Are you satisfied?"

"Yes."

The fire engine circled the plane once and then moved away. It was not by any means a routine operation. Among the firemen was a disguised army officer whose mission was to do some reconnaissance.

Persons who were closer to Dubai were trying to get there as quickly as possible. Among those who joined Hideo Kyōno and Takanori Kitahara were: from Kuwait, Kōichi Kimura, first secretary of embassy and chargé d'affaires, and Douglas Hayes from

JAL's branch office; from Tehran, Motoomi Ōba, manager of JAL's office, and dispatcher Yasushi Igarashi; from JAL's Beirut office, Ken Nakajima, manager of the cargo section.

Douglas Hayes would play an important role in events, for he was fluent in English and Arabic, the latter his mother's language. As sales manager in Kuwait, he was second only to the branch manager, and having worked for JAL for ten years, he also had a working knowledge of Japanese. Just as he was ready to depart from Dubai, he received a call from Paddy Flack at Heathrow, who told him, "Charter any plane you can find. Send the bill to me." Hayes was the first JAL employee to reach Dubai.

Yasuyoshi Egawa was on a business trip to Abu Dhabi. He had been assigned in May of the previous year to C. Itoh and Company's office in Bahrain, and he and his family were just getting accustomed to the high temperatures and moisture of the desert climate. As he was about to go to bed, the telephone in his hotel room rang. Toshihiro Nagayama, the manager of the Bahrain office, told Egawa about the hijack and asked him to get to Dubai as soon as he could to help rescue the passengers. Egawa was, Nagayama said, to send him a list of necessary relief goods, which he would purchase and send to Dubai. Egawa dressed quickly and found an Arab driver.

As they drove along the paved road through the desert at a constant speed of sixty-five miles per hour, the air tasted cool and sweet. It was the first time Egawa had breathed such cool air since coming to the Arabian Peninsula. In the glare of the headlights, he caught sight of the bleached bones of a camel.

It was only a little after dawn when he arrived at his destination, but as he made his way through the city, he was stopped and questioned frequently by armed soldiers, on the alert for comrades of the hijackers who might try to cross the desert.

Reporters, both Japanese and foreign, also made their way to

Dubai from Europe and the Arab countries. There were eventually seventy-eight of them, including Arab journalists.

For a while, the only news source had been the London branch office, where Yūsuke Fukada was having a very difficult time answering questions, while at the same time trying to arrange flights for the journalists. Fukada was a neat dresser and usually he would not think of loosening his tie, but when the reporters were gone for a moment, he would sigh with relief and loosen it. But as soon as they came back, he tightened his tie. What he was most worried about was his clothing, which was soaked with perspiration, for he had had no chance to return home for a change of clothes. To a man like Fukada, this was almost unbearable. He imagined the passengers imprisoned in the plane and muttered to himself, "I couldn't stand it if I were one of them."

Contradictory Analyses

The JAL-Hijack Countermeasures Liaison Headquarters called its first meeting at 1:10 P.M. The headquarters, under the chairmanship of Minister of Transport Shintani, was established on the seventh floor of the Ministry of Transport in the office of the chairman of the Air Accidents Investigation Committee. (The complete list of members is shown in figure 2.)

Just as at the meeting held that morning and for the same reasons, no conclusions were reached. The hijackers' purpose was still completely unknown. There were no Israelis among the passengers, nor were there any well-known politicians, businessmen, industrialists or high-ranking government officials who might be particularly valuable as hostages. The only person of some note was Professor Akira Shōda, whom the hijackers did not seem to consider an effective instrument in their bargaining; it was not clear whether they even knew that he was a cousin of the crown princess.

What was considered likely was that, because it had been a Japanese plane, there would be demands made to the Japanese government. Japan maintains diplomatic relations with both Israel and the Arab states, but it is neither an ally of the former nor an enemy of the latter. Thus it was not thought that the demands would be political in nature.

Still in the dark about the situation in Dubai, the headquarters considered various demands that might be made. One possibility was that the hijackers would demand ransom money, as had been the case in the Lufthansa incident the previous year. Since they had

Figure 2

JAL-HIJACK COUNTERMEASURES LIAISON HEADQUARTERS

Chairman

Torasaburō Shintani, Minister of Transport

Vice Chairmen

Jūshirō Komiyama, Deputy Director, Public Affairs Section, Prime Minister's Office
Kiyofumi Miyazaki, Deputy Director, Public Affairs Section, Prime Minister's Office
Kiyoshi Mizuno, Parliamentary Vice Minister of Foreign Affairs
Shinsaku Hōgen, Vice Minister of Foreign Affairs
Bunsei Satō, Parliamentary Vice Minister of Transport
Yasuichi Takabayashi, Vice Minister of Transport
Mikio Takahashi, Director General, National Police Agency
Shizuo Asada, President, Japan Air Lines

Members

Akira Watari, Chief, Counselling Section of the Secretariat, Prime Minister's Office
Hideho Tanaka, Director, Middle East and Africa Bureau, Ministry of Foreign Affairs
Nobuyuki Uchimura, Director, Civil Aviation Bureau, Ministry of Transport
Shizuhiko Yamamoto, Director, Security Bureau, National Police Agency
Yasumoto Takagi, Vice President, Japan Air Lines

said that they were acting in cooperation with the Japanese Red Army faction, it was also conceivable that they would demand the release of Japanese activists held in Japanese jails. That they might demand the release of Kōzō Okamoto was considered but rejected. Okamoto, the only survivor of the massacre at Lod Airport, was serving a life sentence in Israel. It is said that he regretted his part in the attack and was engaging in deep self-criticism. Moreover, according to recent reports from Beirut, he had revealed all he knew to Israeli authorities and, consequently, had been branded a traitor by the Palestinian guerrilla organizations.

Reasoning that the incident could be solved more quickly if a government representative was on hand to negotiate directly, Shintani proposed that I be sent to Dubai. This proposal was accepted, but I later came to the conclusion that this decision was an arbitrary one. In retrospect, it seems to have been a violation of the principle of international trust, an aspect that the members of the committee were not aware of at that time.

Another point that did not come out at the meeting was that some members feared that I, as a party politician, might act independently, ignoring the policies of the government. This I later heard from a highly placed bureaucrat. Shinjirō Yamamura had referred to "murmurings from my surroundings," and they were already in the air at this stage. Fortunately, the murmurings did not reach my ears.

I told the members of the committee that since I was going as the government's representative, I had to be fully informed of the fundamental policies of the government. I sought their opinion of what I should do if ransom money was demanded. "Should I promise to pay the full amount or bargain for a reduction?" I asked.

This brought wry smiles to the faces of some of those present; the atmosphere seemed to become a little more relaxed. I heard the following remarks.

"It can't be helped, I think."

"It depends on the amount of money demanded."

"Let's pay whatever is demanded."

The consensus seemed to be to pay ransom money if it were demanded, but I pressed them further. "Even if the amount exceeds one billion yen?"

"The lives of the passengers cannot be evaluated in terms of money. We'll have to swallow their demands," was the reply.

While I could not deny that we were in a tight spot, I thought to myself, "Is it proper and right to decide the payment of such an astronomical sum in such a casual way?"

To the others I said, "It's going to be the first time in my life that I'm going to pay one billion yen to someone. There'll never be another occasion like this," at which everyone burst into laughter–everyone, that is, except the two men from the National Police Agency, whose glum expressions did not change.

I then asked, "What shall I do if the hijackers demand the release of Japanese Red Army leaders imprisoned in Japan? I think such a demand is very likely. If they demand that the leaders be transported to South America or some other place, will a plane be provided?"

Director General Mikio Takahashi of the police agency, speaking in a cautious tone, said, "We'll consider such a situation."

"Consider the situation? That's not enough. I want you to promise that you'll do it," I retorted.

There was no reply.

"If they demand it, I'm going to promise them that it will be done. Is that all right?"

Again there was no immediate reply, but I succeeded in having my proposals agreed to. Since it was not clear what demands might be made, the men from the police agency did not seem much concerned about my statement that I would meet any demands; apparently they were thinking that the problem could be studied after demands were actually made. But I was in dead earnest. If the government did not carry out promises that I made to the hijackers, the consequences would be quite clear and most probably tragic. Thus I wanted to obtain a guarantee from the police agency that promises would be fulfilled.

I then said, "In the event that the hijackers refuse to release the passengers and crew, I would like to offer myself as a hostage," and mentioned the precedent for this. Everyone seemed to have expected this, but it was pointed out that the two cases were different–Japanese radicals in the former and Palestinian guerrillas in the present.

Although the majority was not in favor of putting up a hostage, I was firmly convinced that this should be done if there was even one chance in a thousand of success. After arguing my case forcefully, I finally obtained reluctant agreement to my becoming a hostage in exchange for the passengers. The one man who was especially cool to this proposal was the vice minister of foreign affairs, Shinsaku Hōgen. Turning toward me, he said, "Vice Minister Satō, if you give yourself as a hostage, it'll be the last time we'll ever see you. According to an analysis of the situation by the foreign ministry, there is a possibility that the hijackers may fly the plane over Israel and then blow it up in a *kamikaze* attack on some important area of the country. If you board the plane as a hostage, they'll surely blow it up in a suicide attack."

He seemed to be saying that I was sure to be killed. Perhaps I turned pale at his words. I do not know.

Everyone was looking at me. I searched for words and then replied, "This is the first I have heard of the appraisal by the foreign ministry. But the minute I board the plane, there will be no hesitation on my part. This is not to say that I am indifferent to being part of a suicide attack, but I can't stand aside doing nothing. Even if the passengers were safely evacuated, it would be my duty to rescue the pilot and other members of the crew. I'll do my best to persuade the hijackers to release them."

In a taunting voice, someone demanded, "How do you propose to persuade the hijackers?"

But I was confident. "I'll do it step by step, depending on their attitude. Even terrorists value their own lives. During the process of negotiation, I'll try to persuade them of the value of their lives and come to a compromise by which both theirs and the lives of the hostages can be saved. I'll even promise to bring them to Narita airport."

I did not believe that if I only listened to demands and followed them to the letter negotiations would be successful. I wanted to bring them to Japan, where negotiations would be easier than in a foreign country. For this method to succeed, I knew that I would have to convince the hijackers of my sincerity, but however difficult negotiations might be, I was determined to do my best.

To my listeners, bringing the hijackers to Narita airport seemed preposterous. Again there was laughter, but it was not an idea that had occurred to me suddenly. The airport was ready for use. The thirteen-thousand-foot, north-south runway was completed, men were already undergoing training in the control tower, and lighting equipment was operational. The aprons were designed to accommodate jumbo jets; even the two steel towers erected by antiairport demonstrators at the southern end of the runway did not present an obstacle to aircraft landing or taking off. When an oil pipeline was completed, the airport would be ready for operation.

My remark was not meant to be facetious. I was convinced that Narita was the best place in Japan to carry out negotiations. I thought to myself, "What's odd about bringing them to Narita? We have no choice but to listen to their demands because of the hostages. But isn't it also necessary to find a solution that is favorable to us? I know they are tough and uncompromising, but I'll go to Dubai with the intention of bringing them to Japan." Although I dislike hurting others' feelings, the words on the tip of my tongue were, "What's so funny?" I noticed that the two men from the police agency did not laugh.

I had one more question for them. I said, "If I bring the hijackers to Narita and promise them that we'll let them fly anywhere they want when the whole problem is solved, will you back me up and carry out my pledge?"

"That's impossible. We'll have to arrest them under Japanese law," replied Takahashi.

"You can't do that," I retorted. "There's a possibility that I'll have to bring them to Narita. If that happens, I want to request that you solve the problem not under the Japanese criminal code but politically."

No one replied.

The atmosphere of the meeting suggested a lack of commitment owing no doubt to the absence of demands and the scarcity of information. I myself had a feeling of futility. Only the words of Vice Minister Hōgen to the effect that the plane would be blown up over Israel rang in my ears.

As the meeting ended and I left for my office, Kiyoshi Mizuno, the parliamentary vice minister of foreign affairs, tried to comfort me. "I don't envy your post as parliamentary vice minister of transport," he said. I was happy to hear such words, though they had been said in a light vein. I rather regretted that Yamamura had set the precedent he did.

At the time, I wondered what the assessment of the foreign ministry was based on. I learned later that a priority cable had been received at 7:51 that morning from the Japanese embassy in Tel Aviv. The Israeli government had obtained information that the terrorists were acting in conjunction with the Red Army faction and linking this with the Lod Airport massacre came to the conclusion that a suicidal attack on Israel was at least a possibility. As I mentioned previously, chargé d'affaires Matsufuji was at Lod Airport, and Israeli forces were on alert.

Returning to my office, I sat down at my desk. Although ordinarily I would pay little attention to it, my eyes came to rest on the telephone. The number ended in "4274," which could be pronounced as either *shini nashi* or *shinin nashi*. Either pronunciation could be interpreted to mean, "No one will die." I hoped that it was a good omen–no one will die!

Defense Minister Rashid was putting pressure on the hijackers. There is an Arab saying that goes, "Bread in one hand and a sword in the other." This fitted Rashid perfectly. He called Kassay.

"Carmel, how was the food I sent you?"

"It was delicious. I'd like to thank you for your kindness on behalf of all the persons on board."

"I'm happy to hear you found the food delicious. Do you want anything else?"

"I can never thank you enough for your magnanimity. I don't want to impose on your kindness too much, but I have one more request to make. Will you hear me?"

"Please feel free to speak. I'll do anything in my power."

"The water you sent us became very hot because of the temperature outside when it was delivered. We find it hard to drink. Could you send us some ice?"

"I didn't think about that. My apologies. We'll send you the ice right away, together with some fruit."

"Thank you very much."

"Could you answer my question? Are you an Arab like me?"

"Yes, I am. I'm a Palestinian and a commando."

"It's good to hear that. Then I presume that you understand the Koran, which tells us to give to the poor and to the hungry. I'd like you to understand that I am only following the teachings of the Koran."

"I understand perfectly."

"Thank you. After the ice and fruit have been sent to you, I'd like to talk with you as two persons who understand the Arab spirit. Will you do that?"

"Yes, I'll agree to that."

"Then we'll talk later."

After about thirty minutes, the conversation was resumed.

"I'd like to make a request. Please release the passengers and crew from the plane. Also please disembark yourselves so that we can have a face-to-face talk."

"It's regretful, but that's simply impossible."

"Could you tell me why?"

"I and my comrades are commandos. We have no authority to obey your wishes."

"Then could you release all the women and children aboard the plane?"

"I'm sorry, I can't do that. I don't have the authority. I've already violated my authority by releasing the injured purser. I'll have to report this to my organization later."

"Could you inform me of the name of your organization? I'd like to negotiate directly with them."

"Not now. Time will probably disclose the name of our organization."

"I'd again like to request you to release all the women and children aboard the plane."

"Impossible."

"Have you no love, mercy and compassion in your heart?"

"Don't say such things. I'm just a commando."

"It's very regretful that you can't hear my request. I'll have to inform you of an order issued by the United Arab Emirates. The United Arab Emirates orders you to release all passengers and crew. It orders you to return the plane to Japan Air Lines."

"I ignore your order. If you should try to translate the order into action, we'll blow up the plane. Bombs have been placed at all entrances. I regret that I cannot show the bombs to you. If any of your soldiers should even approach the plane, we'll blow it up.

This is not an idle threat. It is a reply to the order issued by your country. Please retract the order."

"All right. I pray to Allah that your mercy will fall on the passengers."

"Thank you for retracting the order. I'm also an Arab. I have a merciful heart too. But at present I've lost all interest in talking with you."

With that, Rashid was greeted with the silence of a switch suddenly closed.

Ever since the countermeasures meeting, the word *death* had hung heavily over my head. I consider myself an optimist, but now I was not feeling optimistic. I suddenly recalled my trip to the city of Chiba only two days previously, on the evening of July 19.

There was a small group of residents around the airport who were against its being opened, but the prospects were good that they could be persuaded to come to terms if enough time was spent in negotiations. A greater problem was the antagonism of residents along the projected route of the pipeline. That evening, I was to meet with the latter. I planned to listen patiently to their opinions and then express my own on behalf of the ministry.

After we had finally reached agreement in favor of a frank exchange of opinions, the meeting had been planned two months previously. The police in Chiba, however, were not in favor of my going and advised me that it would be dangerous for me to attend because the activities of the antiairport group had become quite vigorous. They did not say in so many words that they could not guarantee my safety, but they were evidently quite worried. Officials within the ministry were also concerned and persuaded me to postpone the meeting to a later date.

I myself became a little apprehensive and thought of not taking Yoichi Furubayashi, my secretary, with me. When I mentioned this to him, a strange look came to his face and he said, "I'm your secretary. It's my job to accompany you anywhere." With that, I gave in.

Furubayashi and I arrived at the apartment house where the meeting was to be held on schedule, at 8 P.M. There was no meeting of minds, but the representatives from the other side did listen to my arguments with patience. There was no danger to my life, and after about two hours, the meeting ended. During the return trip, I felt quite exhilarated, very different from the way I had felt on the way to Chiba.

Ministry chauffeurs are not particularly in the habit of chatting with their passengers, but my driver, Iwao Mitsuhashi, suddenly said, "Mr. Vice Minister, would you like to hear some *naniwabushi*?" (*Naniwabushi* is a particular style of stories that are sung.)

The title of the song that now came from the car stereo was *Mori no Ishimatsu*, in which there is a passage that goes, "A fool, unless he dies, cannot be cured." All during the trip I listened to the song. When we reached my official residence in Kudan, it had not ended, so I asked Mitsuhashi to drive around the block.

Mori no Ishimatsu, a samurai who lived in the nineteenth century, belonged to a group led by Shimizu no Jirōchō. Ishimatsu was famous for his assistance to the poor and his chivalry toward the downtrodden, and he used to go on dangerous missions knowing full well that he was risking his life. Being a good fighter, he usually escaped, but then one day a man who had borrowed money from him arranged a meeting, at which he said he would repay the money. What actually happened was that Ishimatsu was attacked and killed by the man and his cohorts. Ishimatsu is still famous, his exploits appearing not only in song but in movies, on television and on the stage.

Was I, I wondered, like Ishimatsu, a fool for having made the trip to Chiba? (Fortunately the results were contrary to what others had feared.) Mitsuhashi, who knew very well that I was usually fond of listening to light music, had proposed the *naniwabushi*. He himself must have been very fond of this type of story-telling. I did not think, however, that it was a coincidence that he had made the connection with Ishimatsu. He had probably been thinking all along that the trip I was making to discuss the laying of the pipeline was foolhardy.

And now I was going to go to Dubai and would perhaps become a hostage. Might I die a foolhardy death, as Vice Minister Hōgen had intimated? As I recalled the trip to Chiba, I became more and more pessimistic. Nothing that happened that afternoon made the situation any clearer or changed my mood.

I was visited by Yūjirō Koike, an old friend of mine. Koike was president of a company engaged in developing oilfields in the Arab countries. From his home in Beirut, where he lived for about eight months of the year, he traveled around the desert by car and plane. He had many friends among Arab royalty and in political and government circles. I was, of course, glad to talk to someone who was so well informed on Arab affairs. When he heard that we had no idea of the hijackers' intentions, he quickly telephoned a man named Nasser, the secretary general of the Tokyo office of the League of Arab States.

The assistant secretary, Bahei Eldin Nasr, arrived at the Ministry of Transport within half an hour. Nasr's analysis of the situation was explicit. "Only money," he said, "the hijackers want only money. Since there seems to be a Japanese among them, there is a possibility that some demand other than money may be made. But I'm convinced that money is their ultimate objective. They haven't made any demands since landing. This is a case like the Lufthansa hijacking last year, which itself was unlike other cases of hijacking. The hijackers probably belong to the same organization." His opinion was shared by his colleagues in the Tokyo office.

I asked him about the problem that had been troubling me. "Do you think there is any possibility that the hijackers will carry out a suicidal attack on an Israeli installation?"

"No," he replied. "The probability is very slight. In the attack at Lod Airport, the terrorists were on the ground, not in a plane. It would be impossible for them to enter Israeli airspace without being shot down. The Israeli Air Force will be on total alert because of the bitter experience at Lod. The hijackers, who I'm sure have fought against the Israeli Army and Air Force in the past, are well acquainted with the striking power of the air force. I don't think they are fools enough to try, knowing that there is little likelihood of reaching their destination."

Here was an opinion quite opposite that of the foreign ministry, which, it seemed to me, was inclined to rely too much on information furnished by Israel and the United States. Their policies, oriented toward the United States, placed more credence in information from Israel, an ally of the United States, than in information from Arab states, which are not as close to the United States. To make matters worse, there was still almost no information from Japanese diplomatic missions in the Arab countries.

Nasr went on to say that "the incident will probably not be solved in Dubai. They'll certainly fly to another airport, in which case it will be either Cairo, Tripoli in Libya, or Aden in the People's Democratic Republic of Yemen."

He did not explain his reasons for making this statement. It seems that the relationship between the Arab states and the Palestinian guerrilla organizations is very delicate and complicated and, for people of other countries, extremely difficult to understand. It should be noted that the common opinion among Arabs living in Tokyo was that Dubai was only a temporary base from which the guerrillas would launch their next operation. Developments would show that there was much truth in this viewpoint.

I made Nasr's analysis known to the foreign ministry, but they adhered to the idea of a *kamikaze* attack. To the countermeasures headquarters, his analysis was only one of many, and there the intention was to solve the matter in Dubai. Nasr had said that the incident was similar to the Lufthansa hijacking, but no one was inclined to pay much attention to this. If we had, the incident would probably have been solved in a different way.

The sole exception was Atsuyuki Sasa, chief of the overseas affairs section of the National Police Agency's Security Bureau. To newsmen who knew him, Sasa was "the man who was always in the middle of any big incident." Among those in which he had been involved were: the demonstration against the entry of the USS *Enterprise* into the port of Sasebo; demonstrations against the establishment of an army field hospital in Hachioji, a suburb of Tokyo; the antiairport demonstrations at Narita; student demonstrations at the University of Tokyo; and the Asama Red Army faction incident. While serving temporarily with the Japanese consulate general in Hong Kong, he had thought there would be nothing to be involved in there, but it turned out otherwise. Some 140 bodies of former officers and men of the Imperial Japanese Navy were unearthed, and the task of supervising their excavation and sending the remains back to Japan fell to him.

The JAL hijack was the first big incident to come along since he had been promoted to his present position. Later there were to be others: a KLM hijacking, the hijacking of a ferry boat in Singapore and the occupation by terrorists of the Japanese embassy in Kuwait.

Although he had no solid basis on which to make an evaluation, he felt intuitively that there was a similarity between the present case and the Lufthansa hijacking and started at once to search for data concerning the latter. Most unfortunately there was practically none available at that time at the police agency, because the incident had not been at all connected with Japan. All that he was able to learn was that there had been a demand for 5 million dollars for the release of the hostages and that the West German airline had been vague about whether or not it had been paid. Sasa felt that there must have been some secret agreement between the hijackers and the airline that would account for the latter's vagueness. He also felt that the hijackers in Dubai, or their organization, would make a similar demand.

At Tokyo International Airport, more than two hundred reporters had converged on the operations center, where a special room had been set aside for their use. JAL had thoughtfully provided sandwiches and soft drinks; munching and drinking, the reporters plied their trade.

Behind the reporters' room was the countermeasures headquarters, in a room normally used by JAL's executive director, Hiroshi Arai. Thirty telephones had been installed, and circuits were kept open to Europe and other areas of the world. A loudspeaker in one corner allowed others in the room to listen in on the conversations. All information was tape recorded.

Asada was on his way to Bangkok, but all the other top executives of the airline were present, including Vice President Yasumoto Takagi and the top management of the flight division. Information officers, including Yūjirō Hagiwara, chief of the publicity section, listened to developments and gave news to the reporters.

Suddenly the voice coming from the loud-speaker would fade and become inaudible, and all the staff except Takagi and two or three other officials would leave the room. This was an indication that top secret information was being discussed. When the communication ended, they would huddle together and listen to the tape recording.

One reduction in the volume of the loud-speaker was because of particularly chilling information. Douglas Hayes, relaying his message via London, said that if the relief plane landed in Dubai, the hijackers might become excited and use their guns or explode dynamite.

On the basis of this report, the operations center decided that the relief plane should land in Abu Dhabi, but this presented a problem. The area between Abu Dhabi and Dubai is largely desert in which guerrillas could hide and make a surprise attack on the team, which would of course be completely unarmed. Takagi did not want any more hostages to be taken. The operations center ordered Hayes, via London, to send an immediate reply on ways of transporting the relief team between the two cities.

JAL employees from Tehran and Beirut had joined Hayes, and the four men constituted an advance party preparing for the arrival of the relief team–looking for quarters and collecting information. The men from Chūtō Oil, Mitsubishi Trading Company and C. Itoh and Company were also hard at work collecting information. In the ordinary course of events, they would have been engaged in cutthroat competition. Now they were all cooperating and working for a common goal.

Somewhat later, after consultations with Motoomi Ōba, the operations center drafted a plan for transporting the relief team. They were to fly from Abu Dhabi to Ash-Shariqah on Gulf Air flight 339 and go from there to Dubai by road. But just then encouraging news was received from Ōba, who reported that the governments of Dubai and the United Arab Emirates would take the responsibility for transportation. A military transport would be sent to Abu Dhabi to take Asada and some of his team to Ash-Shariqah, from where they would be taken by car to Dubai. The rest of the team would be provided with a bus to take them to Dubai, and in both cases there would be police escorts.

July 21 was coming to an end in Tokyo.

Toward Dubai

The relief plane was soon to take off from Bangkok, destination unknown.

Sandwiches and a special Japanese dish known as *suzume-zushi* were loaded aboard the plane. If the latter could be gotten to the captive passengers, they would at least know that a relief team had arrived from Japan. But permission to land in Dubai had not been received. Without permission, the plane could not land. Asada realized how difficult it was to negotiate with a country with which Japan did not have diplomatic relations.

Yoshiyasu Mayumi had sent the following message to Tokyo at 7:35 P.M. (Japan time), about two hours after the plane had landed: "The first plan is to fly directly to Dubai, but in case we do not obtain permission, or in case it is difficult to land there due to unfavorable conditions, we would like to fly to either Abu Dhabi, Bahrain or Karachi. We had hoped to depart Bangkok at 7:35 JST but we will be a little late."

From Tokyo, JAL urged London to "hurry contact with Dubai. Do all you can to obtain entry permission for the relief plane. Report back as soon as you have succeeded."

The man on the spot was Douglas Hayes, who went to a certain official in the Dubai government and pleaded passionately for permission for the plane and the relief team to enter the country. At the same time, granting entry permission to Hayes as an individual did not mean that the plane could fly directly to Dubai. To make the permission valid, a Japanese diplomatic mission would have to contact the government of Dubai through a third country. Only after such a procedure could Dubai inform Japan that the right to enter had been officially granted.

Hayes knew all this, but he continued to plead with the official. He also kept in close contact with Amar Biji, the information officer at the airport. From this source, he relayed the following information at about noon (5:30 P.M. in Japan): "There has been no definite change in the situation. The hijackers have not presented any demands as yet. They say they are waiting for 'instructions.' Rashid is shaking his head and saying, 'I haven't heard of an attitude like this being taken by any hijackers in the past.' We have informed them that we will provide any medical assistance necessary for the passengers. If they request permission to take off, we'll grant it. But they haven't demanded refueling as yet. Employees of BOAC are standing by in case this demand is made."

About ten minutes later, London relayed a message saying that "according to information broadcast by Radio Tel Aviv, the Dubai government will not make any responsible reply to any demand made by the hijackers before JAL President Asada arrives. We do not know how Radio Tel Aviv obtained this information, but if it is true, we believe that entry permission will be granted for the JAL plane or any other relief plane from other airlines."

Although the reliability of this information was in doubt because of its source, it was relayed to Asada and judgment was left up to him. He decided it was better not to stay in Bangkok; they would fly toward Dubai and depend on information received in flight. Accordingly, he indicated to chief pilot Asama that the flight plan should list Abu Dhabi as the first place to land, but if circumstances permitted, they would fly to Dubai, the final to decision be made after receiving word from Tokyo.

The relief plane took off at 9:21 P.M. (Japan time). Asama's flight plan called for flying 1,110 miles in a northwesterly direction to arrive over Calcutta; to fly from there for 1,360 miles in a west-northwesterly direction to arrive over Karachi; to fly from there for 800 miles over the Arabian Sea to arrive in Abu Dhabi. Flight time would be six and one half hours. If Dubai became the destination, a course change 8 degrees north of Karachi would be made. In either case, the flight time from Karachi would be one and one half hours.

From BOAC's office in Kuwait, the message was that "the routes over Syria and Saudi Arabia have been closed due to the hijack. Be careful!" It appeared therefore that Asada had no alternative to landing in either Abu Dhabi or Dubai.

It was while the plane was over India that Hayes learned from the Dubai government that permission to land had been granted, and this information was relayed to the Ministry of Foreign Affairs by First Secretary Kimura. Hayes's report said, "Entry visas for President Asada and his relief team will be issued after they arrive in Dubai. This is to be considered a special case. The government of Dubai has given permission for the plane to land in Dubai. I have expressed, on behalf of JAL, our deep gratitude for the magnanimity of the Dubai government. According to the government, the hijackers are prone to become very excited at even minor happenings. We are worried about what they will do if they see the relief plane landing in Dubai. . . ."

The relief plane was over Karachi when this information reached it. Asada did not hesitate one minute in selecting Abu Dhabi as the place to land, even if it meant delaying their arrival in Dubai slightly.

It seemed to Hayes that the wide chasm between Dubai and Japan had shrunk considerably. But it was still there.

Notwithstanding that the plane was fast approaching Dubai, all messages had to travel around the globe, from Dubai to London to Tokyo to the plane. As they flew on, cutting through the skies

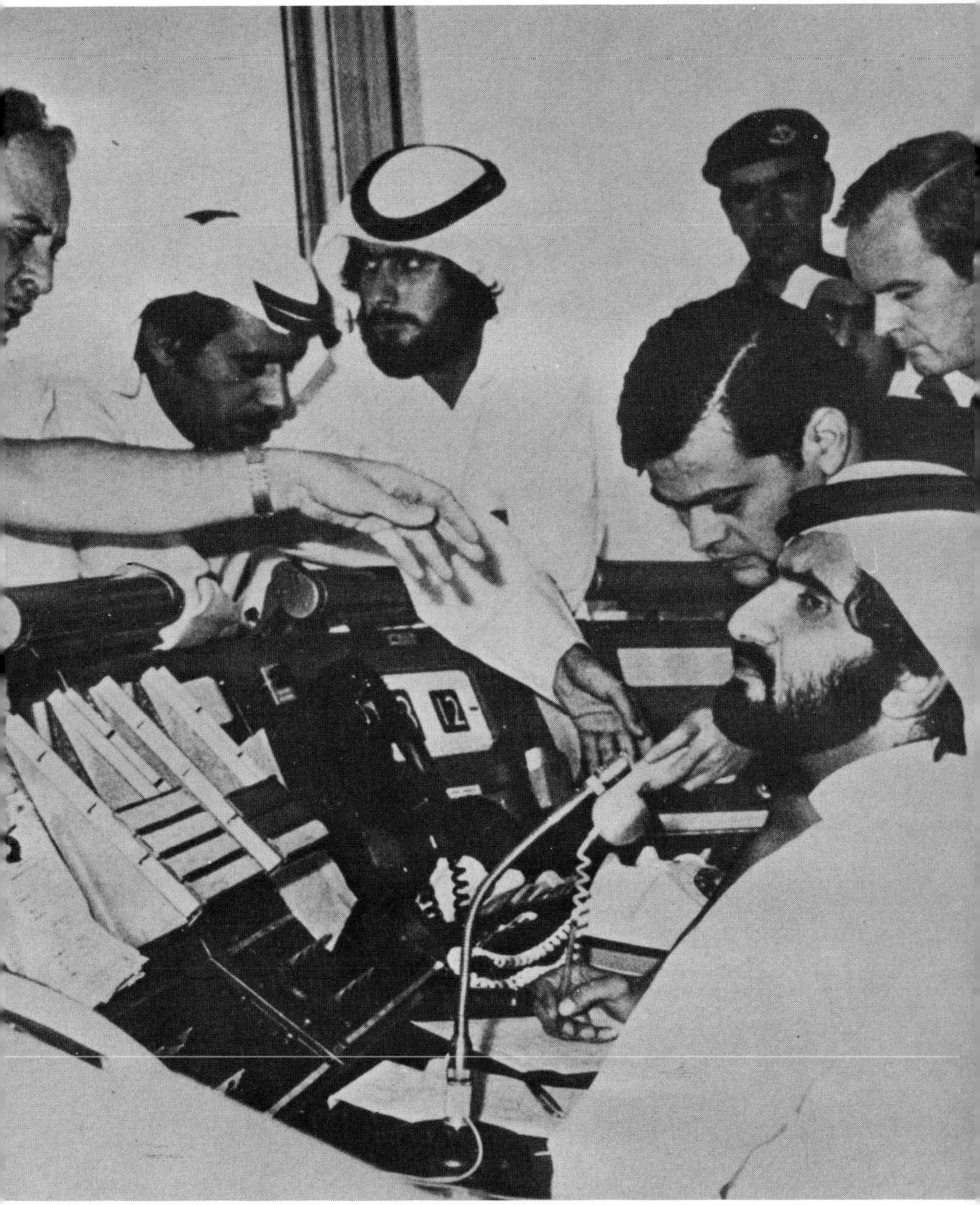

The Dubai control tower; at right, Sheikh Rashid.

View of Dubai Airport after JAL plane landed on July 21, 1973.

Officials of the sheikhdom of Dubai and the United Arab Emirates.

Troops ready for action, Dubai Airport, July 23, 1973.

Destruction of JA8109 at Baninah Airport, Benghazi, July 24, 1973.

Passengers and stewardess immediately after their release.

Hijackers as sketched by a passenger.

above the Arabian Sea, Asada thought that the jet engines had taken on a more powerful note.

The plane settled down on the runway at Abu Dhabi and came to a stop at 10:32 P.M. local time. Eight minutes later it was parked in front of the terminal. The first destination had been reached, but the hijack incident was far from over.

On the plane, the passengers had finished their evening meal, the third provided by the government of Dubai.

A night and a day lay between the captives and Amsterdam, and a feeling of resignation was spreading among them. The hijackers continued to order everyone to hold up his hands; everyone had to obtain permission to leave his seat. Naoko, who was allowed to roam freely, was the only exception, and it may be said that this was the only humanistic act on the part of the terrorists.

Among the passengers were ten employees of JAL. Motohiko Furuichi and two of his colleagues in the communication and management section were on their way back to Tokyo from Paris, where they had attended a conference on information systems. Furuichi's younger brother, Fumihiko, was also on board, returning from Algeria, where he had been since 1970 as an employee of the Japan Benzine Company. The brothers had met in Paris.

"As a staff member of JAL," Furuichi was thinking, "isn't there something I can do?" He came to the conclusion that he should be the calmest person among the passengers and, in case of an emergency, assist the crew in all possible ways.

Kassay, though he was unaware of it, had been given the nickname "Red Shirt" by his captives, simply because he was wearing a red shirt. By this time, it had become pretty dirty.

Rashid and Kassay resumed their talks. (Rashid had not once left the control tower.)

"Are you comfortable in the plane? What's the temperature? It's

100 degrees outside. The humidity is 85 percent. The heat is very oppressive."

"I'm sorry to hear that. The temperature is being maintained at 74–80 degrees. I'd like to make a request in order to maintain this temperature. Will you listen to me?"

"I was going to ask you about the same thing. Please make your request."

"According to the crew, if we continue using the air conditioning, the plane's batteries will soon run down. Could you arrange to recharge the batteries?"

"That's exactly what I was worrying about. There's no vehicle here equipped with a recharger, but I've found out that BOAC has one. Would you like to borrow it?"

"I don't want to trouble BOAC, but I see no other way. Could you ask BOAC on my behalf?"

"Okay. I'm sure they will gladly lend us the vehicle for the sake of the passengers."

"I'm very grateful."

"Could you listen to my request?"

"Anything within my power. I believe I'll have to do something to repay your kindness."

"I'm happy to hear that. My request concerns the passengers. Won't you release them? If you can't release all, could you at least free the women and children?"

"I don't have the authority to do that."

"What should be done in order to obtain their release?"

"Nothing. I simply can't do as you request."

"You haven't made any demands. . . . You refuse to release the passengers. . . . You're just sitting on the runway doing nothing. . . . What is your objective?"

"We're only waiting for instructions from our organization."

"Both the PLO and the PFLP have stated that they have nothing to do with your actions. Are you really Palestinian guerrillas? I'm beginning to think that you are not soldiers–just bandits. Isn't it true that you're ordinary bandits?"

"You'll achieve nothing by provoking me or making me angry. I'm not a person to be influenced by anger. I'm warning you now. We've placed sticks of dynamite at strategic places. They can be set off anytime we choose. Time will tell whether we're soldiers or bandits."

"I'm looking forward to that time. I fervently hope that you are not bandits but soldiers with great pride. I don't like to talk with bandits."

"You won't be disappointed."

"Won't you at least tell me the name of the organization to which you belong? It'll be known sooner or later."

"We've already discussed this. The time has still not arrived to disclose it, although, as you say, it'll be known sooner or later. If the name is to be disclosed, it will be done by our organization itself."

"I understand. I'll retract my question. I want to protest now the fact that you won't even release a single child."

"I'd like to apologize to you as an individual. This is my true feeling."

"I'll remember your feeling. I want to have a talk with you again before you go to sleep. Could you promise to talk with me?"

"Yes, I'll do that. I want to take a rest now. Light up the area around the plane, will you?"

"Yes."

The ramp used in delivering food was separated from the plane and moved about sixty feet away, as demanded by the hijackers. The doors were locked from the inside.

When I returned home on the night of July 21, I began cleaning out the drawers of my desk, as much to try to hide my complicated feelings as for any other reason. I had already cleaned out my desk at the ministry.

I was glad my wife chose not to say anything. We had been married twenty-eight years, my oldest son was already married, and my two younger sons had graduated from college. After being married for that length of time, a husband and wife find it unnecessary to speak to find out what the other is thinking. As she was silently repacking my bags, the whiteness of the underwear brought a vision of death to my mind. It occurred to me that she too was thinking that I might die, and I felt a great surge of pity for her.

Suddenly she spoke. "Are you going to leave without calling your mother?"

I had not called anyone, neither my closest friends or relatives. If Vice Minister Hōgen had not spoken so ominously, I probably would have called up all my friends in a fit of heroism. But with death looming over me, I simply could not do it.

Whenever I was in deep trouble, it was my habit to try and look at myself objectively and then write a *waka* (a poem in thirty-one syllables) to express what I felt about my self-reflection. I now felt as if I was in deep trouble, but because of the rising tension, I could not stand still. Was I, I wondered, a coward? To bolster my spirits, I scolded myself, shouting, "and you say you're a politician!" But my sagging spirits continued to sag. I felt ashamed.

If I were to telephone anyone in that frame of mind, I would go on talking endlessly and probably say that I had made up my mind to take on the mission regardless of what happened. Words of bravado, yes, but I knew they would not express my true feelings. So I called no one.

I did receive a great number of calls, some from complete strangers, encouraging me and expressing the hope that my mission would be a success. I conversed as calmly as I could, in spite of the apprehension gripping my heart. In retrospect, after the incident had been solved, I feel that I was foolish to have been so worried, but at the time I did not know what lay ahead.

At 11 o'clock the next morning, I got around to calling my eighty-one-year-old mother, who lives with my sister on the southern island of Kyushu. She said only, "Go and do your job," not even adding that I should take good care of myself.

"She's as strong willed as ever," I thought to myself. Some thirty years earlier when I was inducted into the army and sent to Manchuria, her words of farewell had been equally brief. When I returned from the war, my sister told me that every day, from the day I was drafted, my mother had prayed at the Shinto shrine, come rain or shine, for my well-being.

Later I learned from my sister that after I left Tokyo, my mother stayed up late every night, watching news of the hijack on television, and though she was fond of her grandchildren, whenever there was hijack news, she would not let them change the channel.

Her words reminded me of what a strange thing human emotions are; instantly when I heard them, the feeling that I might be a coward vanished. But the change in my feelings was strange even to me. I must have been completely overwhelmed by her spiritual strength. At any rate, I appreciated her brevity. I perceived in her the blood of her samurai ancestors, for she had been born in the Meiji period (1868–1912), the daughter of a former chief retainer of the Kizuki clan in Kyushu. My older sister, whom I called right after talking to my mother, was born in the next reign (Taisho, 1912–26); she wept throughout our conversation.

I had left my official residence about two hours before calling my mother. As I got into the car, I looked up at the fourth floor, where I could see my wife at the window; I waved to her. Other members of the Diet living on the same floor waved and shouted, "Be careful."

Soon after reaching the ministry, the second meeting of the countermeasures committee was convened. I reported on my meeting with Nasr.

It was pointed out that if the plane left Dubai and landed in Tripoli, Libya, or some other airport, the rescue operation would face numerous, perhaps insurmountable, difficulties. As a consequence of this, I was told to go and solve the problem in Dubai and nowhere else. I was not to give the hijackers one single drop of fuel.

Needless to say, it was my intention to do just that, but if the hijackers threatened to blow up the plane with the crew and passengers still on board, what should I do?

To make matters worse, a man from the foreign ministry offered the opinion that "it would be a debacle if the plane were flown to Aden. That is a country that even diplomats find difficult to enter. Moreover, once one is in the country, it is difficult to get out. The plane must not be flown to Yemen. You must solve the problem in Dubai and Dubai alone."

The People's Democratic Republic of Yemen, whose population of 1.4 million is about one-twentieth that of Egypt, has the same number of universities as the latter. Six of the seven universities are for the training of teachers; the other is an institute of technology. Education is widespread, and the people are not only highly nationalistic but are sympathetic to the Arab guerrillas. Since there were no diplomatic relations between Yemen and Japan, the Ministry of Foreign Affairs would find it difficult to carry out negotiations.

Afterwards, I thought the man was exaggerating, to urge me on to a quick solution, but at the moment I was angry. Minister Shintani was aware of this and after the meeting said to me, "Don't worry about him. Leave it up to me and do your best. But don't do anything rash!"

His words calmed me a bit, and I gratefully accepted both his sympathy and personal farewell gift of two hundred thousand yen.

Returning to my office, I held a press conference, during which I mentioned Shintani's gift, without disclosing the amount. One of the reporters said, "I hope it doesn't become condolence money."

The words *condolence money* startled me, and just then my niece came into the room carrying a large bouquet of flowers. "What is this," I thought, "a joke? Does she think I'm going off on a sightseeing trip?"

Written on the card, however, was "Congratulations on Your Birthday." Birthday? I had completely forgotten. Was it a coincidence that I was leaving on my birthday, or was it an ominous sign?

By the time I left for the airport, my heart was again heavy. On the way, I stopped at the Pacific Hotel in Shinagawa, where members of the passengers' families were gathered. I tried to comfort them, and in turn the imploring look in their eyes inspired and cheered me up. (After I left, some of them were heard to say that I was going only for the effect it would have on my next election.)

The scene at the airport was what one might expect at the height of the summer travel season; moreover it was a Sunday. There were smiles everywhere, on the faces of those arriving and those departing, on the faces of those greeting others and those seeing others off. No one seemed to be giving a solitary thought to a hijacking. We alone were meditative. Many of the captive passengers must have left from a similar setting.

With me were Akira Otokodake of the Civil Aviation Bureau and eight newsmen who regularly covered the Ministry of Transport. We boarded a Swissair flight that was leaving at 2 P.M. There was much laughter inside the plane, too, particularly from a group of young girls from a cooking school. With their teacher Gyosai Tamura, who is rather famous and gives cooking lessons on television, they were off to Europe to sample the distinctive cuisines of several countries.

"Our plane might be hijacked," remarked one of the girls.

"That would be an interesting experience," replied another. They chattered like this without a sign of fear on their faces.

Settling back in my seat, I took out a memo pad and wrote a short poem: "A second farewell to my mother/Then we take wing/for the skies over Dubai." My mind was set; nothing would stand in the way of my carrying out my mission.

The first farewell had taken place in 1941, and I realized that I might not return alive. I was prepared to die then, even if I cannot say that I was not afraid to die. Now I was no longer an army officer under orders, but rather the voluntary representative of the government. I had been a member of the Diet for eight years, but this was the first time that I had been entrusted with such grave authority. I was under heavy pressure to do my duty but at the same time knew that if I became a hostage, my life would be in jeopardy. I confess that I found it difficult to concentrate on the task that lay ahead.

Suddenly I recalled that Shinjirō Yamamura's mission had been a success. I decided I must follow his example. If the terrorists agreed to my proposal, the passengers would probably be released; then the minister of transport and the president of JAL could take over. There was nothing more to worry about.

The relief plane was equipped with special communications equipment enabling Asada to get messages from Tokyo, London and other places. On a regular commercial flight, such facilities were not, of course, available to me. So I planned to disembark in Hong Kong to see if there were any instructions. If there were none, I had to continue on to my next destination. This would increase the time required to get to Dubai, but there was no alternative.

When I arrived in Hong Kong, there had been no change in the situation. (It was rumored that I got off the plane in Hong Kong to contact the hijackers' organization and pay ransom money, but this was not true.) I was still worried about the plane's leaving Dubai, so before I boarded a BOAC flight an hour later, I cabled the government, "Please instruct Dubai not to let the plane take off before I arrive."

It was 10:40 P.M. local time when I arrived (an hour behind schedule) at Bangkok's Don Muang Airport. Ambassador Manri Fujisaki was waiting for me. His report was that no demands had been made, either to the Japanese government or to Japan Air Lines. I left an hour later. The only thing I could do now was go on to Dubai, via Bahrain and Abu Dhabi.

Before he left Tokyo, Asada ordered Takagi to make ransom money available, feeling that the terrorists' objective was not just political. He was, in fact, in possession of secret information to the effect that airlines had paid ransom to Palestinian guerrillas in the past, although the amounts had never been disclosed.

Takagi ordered the London branch to obtain 5 million dollars in cash and requested the Bank of Tokyo to lend 5 million dollars. The London branch, however, was able to obtain only 2 million dollars, and the Bank of Tokyo, only 1 million. Takagi then ordered JAL's New York branch to procure the rest of the money, while the Bank of Tokyo began canvassing for dollars in the United States and Hong Kong.

As it turned out, Asada was quite right in thinking that the hijackers had something besides politics in mind.

At about the time I had left my official residence that morning, Al Harja, the chief cook at the Carlton International Hotel in Dubai, woke up suddenly. It was 4 A.M. No one had awakened him. A few minutes later he went to the hotel kitchen, where he ran into the night manager and learned that the relief team had brought meals for the passengers. "You don't have to prepare breakfast this morning," he was told.

Harja did not linger; he returned to his room and went back to sleep. The day before he had overseen the preparation of two hundred breakfasts, two hundred lunches and two hundred dinners. He was completely exhausted. It was the first time that the hotel had served six hundred meals in one day.

In Abu Dhabi, seven members of the relief team had boarded a small military plane from Dubai, which had been waiting for them. With Asada were Tonao Senda, Katsuya Nohara and Yoshiyasu Mayumi from JAL; Toshirō Oguchi from the foreign ministry; Shigeya Gotō from the Ministry of Transport; and Akira Ishizaki from the police agency. Within a matter of minutes they were on their way to Ash-Shariqah, the sheikdom bordering Dubai on the north. From there they went by road and arrived in Dubai at 12:30 A.M., July 22.

One hour and forty minutes later, Mayumi was able to place a telephone call directly to Tokyo. He said, "We talked with the Dubai government spokesman as soon as we arrived. President Asada is scheduled to hold a conference with Defense Minister Rashid. There is no change in the situation. Visa problems as well as accommodations have all been taken care of through the generosity of the Dubai government."

From Tokyo came the message that "UN Secretary General Waldheim has told us that he is willing to fly to Dubai to solve the hijack if we request him. What is President Asada's opinion?" Mayumi said, "We'll consult with Dubai and then give you a reply. A hot-line will be in operation here from 7 A.M. local time." The conversation lasted only five minutes.

Asada was standing in front of the terminal building, from where he could see the plane in the glare of searchlights. Not a sound was to be heard. He would have liked to tell Konuma of his arrival.

While I was on my way to the airport in Tokyo, Asada was conferring with President Zaid and Prime Minister Rashid Al-Maktoum. The president and Asada went to the control tower, and the president made the following analysis: "The hijackers are following a strategy that does not conform to the pattern in any previous incident. More than twenty-four hours have elasped since they landed here, yet they have demanded nothing except food and water.

"It may be that the woman who was killed was their leader and that she was the only person familiar with details of the plan. Her death may have created a vacuum among the hijackers, who now do not know what to do next. They say that they are waiting for instructions, but there is no indication that their organization has given them any instructions."

It was obvious that President Zaid also thought that the terrorists were going to be extremely difficult to deal with. What was unknown at the time was that someone had sent a letter to the airline setting forth demands.

The Blackmail Letter

From the chronological point of view, the place of the blackmail letter in the Dubai incident is ambiguous, but that is not all. The letter has not been fully explained, even today. There are several points unresolved, and I believe that at best it will take some time for them to be completely clarified. It is possible, though, that the letter will remain a mystery.

The people who first read the letter simply could not believe it, so absurdly overdramatic did it seem to them. The feeling they had was that of watching an imported movie of the thriller variety. It must be, they thought, the work of a prankster. (Pranksters, if they can be called that, were on the fringes of the incident later on.)

That the letter did not reach Japan Air Lines until shortly before noon on July 23 was certainly contrary to the terrorists' timetable. (Even today, radical groups adamantly maintain that the letter was held up because of "demogoguery and scheming" on the part of JAL and the police; this, of course, is firmly denied by both parties.) The reason that it did not arrive on time would seem to be a simple mistake that took place at the Central Post Office.

To understand what probably happened, we have to turn back the hands of the clock to the morning of July 21. The sorting of mail at Tokyo Central Post Office begins at 8 A.M. and ends at noon. The letters sorted then are those posted within the CPO's collection area (Chiyoda Ward) between 8:30 of the previous evening and about 10:30 that morning; letters posted at the CPO itself by noon are also sorted and canceled.

On that day, mail for domestic delivery bore the cancellation "Tokyo Central 48.7.21 8–12" (forty-eighth year of Showa, July 21, 8 A.M. to noon). Only in the case of overseas mail is the cancellation in Roman letters.

The blackmail letter was cancelled in Roman letters on the morning of July 21, indicating that it was mailed a little before or within twelve hours after the hijack, which occurred at 11:55 P.M., July 20, Japan time.

The postage on the envelope consisted of three stamps: one 100 yen, one 90 yen and one 55 yen, 245 yen altogether. Why the sender, or senders, used such a large amount of postage is not clear. Twenty yen would be enough for an ordinary domestic letter, and for special delivery, 90 yen would be sufficient. If the letter had been intended for a foreign address, which obviously it was not, the rates would have been no more than 110 yen for an ordinary air mail letter or 210 yen for special delivery. The amount of postage was indeed strange.

One might be inclined to think that the letter had been mailed by a foreigner who did not know what Japanese postal rates were. But would guerrillas leave such an important job up to someone unfamiliar with Japan? (I must admit that there seem to be many Japanese who do not know about such matters. I once asked a group of college students if they knew the domestic postal rates. Out of ten students, only one did.) So while the amount of postage is of little help in determining whether the person who posted the letter was Japanese or a foreigner, it does indicate that either careful planning was neglected for this important job, or the one who posted the letter was careless.

The address typed on the envelope in English was:

"URGENT & PERSONAL
"Director
"Japan Air Lines Company L.T.D

"Daini Tekko Bldg. 1–8–2 Marunouchi
"Chiyoda-ku,
"Tokyo."

Here was another example of bad planning or carelessness: The Daini Tekko Building is the location not of JAL's head office but of the main Tokyo branch office. The head office, which is next to the Central Post Office, is in the Tokyo Building and the address is Marunouchi 2–6–3. This is on the west side of Tokyo Station, whereas the Daini Tekko Building is on the other side (Yaesuguchi); to get from one place to the other by the shortest route is little more than a five-minute walk.

It is undeniable that the letter was strategically of great importance and that the sender desired that it reach President Asada (who, incidentally, would not be addressed as "Director") as quickly as possible. The contradiction between this and the address and postage leads me to believe that the men entrusted with the task were easy-going, or, perhaps, just plain sloppy.

It is usual for the Central Post Office to begin distribution of mail received before noon on the afternoon of the same day. In the case of a letter bearing an address within the CPO's delivery area, it is all but certain to be delivered the same afternoon. Why then did JAL not receive the letter until the twenty-third?

After I returned to Japan, the CPO gave me the following explanation: "Because the address was typed in English and because of the large amount of postage, the clerk must have thought that it was bound for a foreign country and, consequently, sorted it into the mail going to the post office at Tokyo International Airport. When the mail was sorted there, it was discovered that the address was domestic, and it was returned to the Central Post Office. As evidence, there is the cancellation mark in Roman letters, which is used only for overseas mail, and over this there is a second cancellation mark, reading 'Tokyo Central 48.7.22 12–18.' From this it can be assumed that the letter was sent back to the CPO on the morning of the twenty-second, sorted before 6 P.M. the same day, and delivered on the morning of the twenty-third."

This is an adequate explanation. On a percentage basis, the mis-sorting of mail is rare, but it is a mistake that does happen from time to time. What a strange coincidence that it should happen to that particular letter! If it had not happened, the incident would probably have been solved sooner and the passengers freed sooner, because it appears that while the hijackers were waiting in Dubai, others were scheduled to contact the airline and relay information on the outcome of that. This would explain why Kassay was repeatedly saying that he was "waiting for instructions." As it was, the Japanese government and Defense Minister Rashid were kept in the dark, and Kassay was in a state bordering on total frustration.

One person who claimed that the letter had been purposely delayed was Fusako Shigenobu, a former leader of the Japanese Red Army faction. Considering that she had fled Japan for an undisclosed Arab country to participate in the Palestine liberation movement, the veracity of her claim seemed quite strong. Her claim was made known to Yoshiko Yamaguchi, a former movie star who entered politics and is now a member of the House of Councillors. Yamaguchi somehow managed to contact the guerrilla leader in her hideout, and the interview was shown on an afternoon television program in Japan.

Shigenobu's story: "On July 21 at 9:30 in the morning, the letter was taken to the reception area of JAL's Marunouchi head office by one of my comrades. There were three desks in the reception area, and when one of the girls left her seat for some reason or other, my comrade placed the letter on her desk. Another comrade then called the JAL office a little after 10 o'clock and ordered them to open the letter, read it and act according to the instructions contained in the letter.

"JAL's claim that the letter was held up because of an error on the part of the post office is preposterous; it's simply a ruse on the part of the airline company."

Shigenobu was perfectly correct about the number of desks, and since she was not in Japan at that time, her claim must have been based on a report she received. If she were to be believed, it would have to be assumed that the airline and the post office were misrepresenting the situation, but the speculation does not end there.

In the Shinjuku area of Tokyo there is a bar called *P*, and among the hostesses who work there, there is one who has numerous acquaintances among the activists and radical students who come in occasionally for a drink. Shigenobu probably does not know the girl, but according to a man who knows the girl quite well, Shigenobu's claim "does not hold water."

His story: "Please remember that what I have to say is only a rumor.

"The blackmail letter, as Shigenobu says, was to have been delivered directly to the JAL head office. But the man who carried the letter became jittery as he approached the office. He didn't enter the building. He bought postage stamps, pasted them on the envelope, and dropped the letter into a mailbox.

"He couldn't report to Shigenobu that he had become frightened and had not delivered the letter directly. He had no alternative but to report that he did what was orginally planned.

"Shigenobu believed the report and told Yamaguchi that the letter had been delivered by one of her comrades. To make it more realistic, the man had even given details on the number of desks. Shigenobu didn't tell Yamaguchi, but the report also contained the information that three police cars had rushed to the head office five minutes after the letter was delivered."

It is difficult to believe the story in its entirety, but, even if it is a rumor, there is something in it that seems to me to contain some truth. The carrier's fright might, for example, explain the unnecessary postage. Still, as I said earlier, what actually happened has yet to be revealed.

The contents of the letter, though explicit, also raised questions. The entire letter, including errors in spelling and typing, is reproduced in figure 3. (The two prisoners, Matsuda and Matsuura, whose release is demanded, were arrested while engaged in the so-called Operation M, the objective of which was to obtain funds by robbing Japanese banks. They had played vital roles since the establishment of the Red Army faction and were in close touch with Shigenobu when she was in Japan. Despite repeated questioning by the authorities, they have never confessed.)

I shall have more to say about the letter at the appropriate time, so for the moment I would like to point out only one of its most puzzling aspects, as well as its apparent connection with the Lufthansa hijacking.

The amount demanded was 3,998,000,000 yen (the equivalent of over 14 million dollars U.S.) in the following currencies:

Yen	1,998,000,000 in 10000-yen notes
U.S. dollars	3,830,000 in 500-dollar bills
French francs	3,880,000 in 500-franc notes
Swiss francs	2,680,000 in 500-franc notes
Deutsche Marks	2,300,000 in 1000-mark notes
Pounds sterling	375,000 in 20-pound notes

Not only is this a very large sum of money, it is bulky–to put it mildly. Banks in Japan generally use large Duralumin trunks for the shipment of currency. Naturally, a full trunk, of say ten-thousand-yen notes, always contains the same amount. Using this for his calculations, Yoshinori Shibata, a section chief at the police agency, figured that to transport only the Japanese yen would require ten trunks. A five-hundred-dollar-bill is smaller than a ten-thousand-yen note (6.6 cm by 15.1 cm as compared to 8.5 cm

URGENT & PERSONAL

Director
Japan Air Lines Company L.T.D.
Daini Tekko Bldg, 1-8-2 Marunouchi
Chiyoda-ku,
Tokyo,
Japan

Dear Sir,

This is to inform you that your Jumbo-Jet, Flight No 404 going from Paris to Tokyo is now under compete control of our commandoes and has landed safely at its pre-planned destination.

The plane, its crew and passengers are now under the complete control of our commandoes who are responsible for their safety. Our commandoes have clear definite instructions to blow up the plane at 13:00 G.M.T. on Monday 23rd July 1973, unless they receive our instructions to the opposite effect. They, according to our orders, will wait until the above mentioned time, and, if they do not receive our instructions to the contrary, they will blow up the plane.

Our organization will release the plane, its crew and passengers provided that you do the following:-

a– Pay a ransom equivalent to the sum of three thousand, nine hundred and ninety eight million Yens. (3,998,000,000–)

and

b– Release Mr. Hisashi Matsuda and Mr. Junichi Matsuura who are prisoners in Japan, and transport them safely to the plane at its destination in Dubai.

If you do not comply, with the following instructions as to the procedures to be taken the plane will be blown up and you will bear full responsibility. You are required to implement the following instructions:-

(1) Your representative should arrive with the ransom at ADEN Airport – People's Democratic Republic of Yemen – at 9:20 G.M.T. Monday 23rd July 1973.

(2) Your representative accompanying with him the two above mentioned persons, should arrive at Dubai Airport at 4:20 G.M.T. Monday

23rd July 1973.

(3) Your representatives may take the plane from Tokyo to Bembay on Sunday 22nd July 1973, according to the following:-

a– Air India (AI) Flight No 301 departing from Haneda Airport at 12:45 local time and arriving at Bmbay Airport 23:35 local time.

b– Swiss Air (SR) Flight No 303 departing from Haneda Airport at 14:00 local time, and arriving at Bombay Airport at 22:40 local time.

(4) Your representative accompanying the two persons will stay at Bombay Airport around four hours in transit before he takes the next plane to Dubai. He may take the following flight:-

a– British Air-line (BA) Flight No 765 departing Bombay Airport at 07:15 local time on Monday 23rd July 1973, and arriving Dubai Airport at 08:20 local time.

(5) Your representative with the two persons will contact the authorities in Dubai to allow him to transport the persons to the plane waiting in Dubai.

(6) Your representative carrying the ransom devided according to the enclosed table, may take the same flight from Tokyo to Bambay and then he will proceed from Bambay to Aden by Air India Flight No 201, departing Bambay Airport at 11:00 local time on Monday 23rd July 1973, and arriving at Airport of Aden at 12:20 local time the same day. He will stay in transit lounge in Bombay Airport around eleven hours.

(7) You will send two other representative carrying similar cases, not containing the ransom, to two other places at the same time :-

a– Kuwait Airport

b– Beirut Airport

(8) Your representative carrying the ransom going to Aden should wear a yellow shirt, black trousers, and should put on black eye glasses, and wear a white hat.

(9) He should carry by himself the cases or case containing the ransom devided according to enclosed table.

(10) Upon arrival at the Aden Airport, your representative, alone and immediately – without contacting anybody by phone or otherwise – should proceed to the parking area outside the Airport:-

a– There he will find a closed car, with a picture of the Arab Revolution Flag on the fron glass. He will proceed toward it.

b– There will be a driver in the car.

c– Your representative should enter the car and sit beside the driver. He should not talk with him at all.

d– Your representative will put the cases on the back seat of the car.

e– He will also put any Arms, Cameras, Recorders, Pens or any such instruments over the suit-cases.

We warn you that he will be seached thoroughly. If any such thing is found on him he will be instantly killed.

(12) Your representative will find further instructions in English in the Tableau of the car in front of him. He should comply with them.

(13) After receiving the ransom we will directly instruct our commandos – who will have already received in the plane at Dubai the two persons mentioned above – to remove all arms and explosives from the plane, and to release it with its crew and passengers.

You have to move in utmost secrecy in following our instructions. The movement of your representatives have to be completely secret. Any deviation from this, and any attempts of any kind to inform the authorities in Japan, Aden or else where, or any attempts to hinder in any way the procedure of delivering the persons and the ransom would result immediately in severing all contacts between us, and you will be held responsible for the results.

We will not be responsible for any damage that will be fall you thereafter.

Let it be known that your representative will be under our continuous watch, control, and protection untill he leaves Aden Airport.

Let it be known that any delay in the arrival of your representative to Aden Airport at the exact time fixed (9:20 G.M.T. Monday 23rd July 1973) will cause immediate severance of all contacts between us and consequently blowing up the plane.

This is the last you hear from us. There will be no further contact between us.

Sons of Occupied Land Organization

Enclosed:- 1– Table of currencies.
2– Small imitation of Arab Revolution Flag.

by 17.5 cm), and the face value is more than ten times greater, so the American currency would require only two trunks. But the total weight of the twelve trunks–for only the Japanese and U.S. currencies–would come to nearly nine hundred pounds.

How could one man, traveling on scheduled airline flights and making stopovers of perhaps four, perhaps eleven hours, be expected to look after more than a dozen trunks weighing well over one thousand pounds? Although there is room for ambiguity in that the instruction may have been meant to pertain only to Aden, the letter says that the representative "should carry by himself the cases or case. . ." (Case?) Conceivably the rules could be stretched so that the two released prisoners could be of assistance, at least part of the way, but what if the government refused to release them? So many questions . . .

Comparing this letter with the one sent to Lufthansa in February, 1972, is revealing, for it establishes without a doubt that the hijackers in both incidents belonged to the same organization. While there are differences in the middle parts where specific instructions are given, the beginning and ending of both letters are all but identical. The Lufthansa letter, also with spelling and typing errors of the original, is reproduced in figure 4.

The Lufthansa jumbo jet, carrying 172 passengers and a crew of 15, was hijacked on February 21, 1972, soon after taking off from New Delhi (bound for Athens). It began with two of the hijackers entering the cockpit and brandishing guns and hand grenades, which was similar to what happened on the JAL flight. There was also a difference in that all women and children were released four hours after the plane landed at Aden airport.

It was shortly after their release that the blackmail letter, which had been mailed, arrived at the airline's head office in Cologne. Preparations to secure the money began immediately. The following is a summary of the incident based on Lufthansa's records.

Figure 4

CONFIDENTIAL & PERSONAL

Director,
DEUTSCHE LUFTHANSA A.G.,
2/6 Von Gablenzstrasse,
D 5 COLOGNE 21,
GERMAN FEDERAL REPUBLIC.

Dear Sir,

This is to inform you that your Jumbo Jet, Flight No. 649 going from New Delhi to Athens is now under complete control of our commandoes and has landed safely at its pre-planned destination.

The plane, its crew and passengers are now under the complete control of our commandoes who are responsible for their safety. Our commandoes have clear definite instructions to blow up the plane at 9.00 GMT on Thursday, 24th February, unless they receive our instructions to the opposite effect. They, according to our orders, have already released all women and children passengers.

Our organisation will release the plane, its crew and the remaining passengers provided that you pay a ransom of five million U.S. Dollars. If you do not comply with the following instructions as to the procedures to be taken the plane will be blown up. You are required to implement the following instructions:-

1- Your representative should arrive at Beirut International Airport at 9.00 GMT on Wednesday, 23rd February, 1972.

2- Your representative may take a private plane from one of the following air charter companies:-
   a) Air Pegasus Hannover GMBH & Co.,
      3 Hannover-Flughafen.

   b) Bavaria Fluggesellschaft Max Schwabe & Co. KG.,
      8 Munchen 87, Flughafen Riem.

   c) ICF- Inter-City-Flug W. Krauss,

4 Dusseldorf; Georg-Glock Strasse 10.

Or he may leave Frankfurt to Jeddah on Tuesday, 22nd February at 23.45 (Local Time) by SV Flight No. 790, then from Jeddah to Beirut on Wednesday, 23rd February at 8.00 (Local Time) by SV 741. He will arrive Beirut International Airport at 9.00.

3– Your representative should wear grey trousers, a black jacket and a white jumper, and should carry in his left hand the News Week Magazine.

4– Your representative should carry in his right hand the case containing the ransom divided according to the enclosed table.

5– Your representative should not be accompanied by any other person.

6– Upon arrival at Beirut International Airport, your representative should proceed alone and immediately- without contacting anybody by phone or otherwise- to the parking area outside the airport (See enclosed plan). There he will find a closed car with the picture of the Lebanese President S. Franjiyeh on the front glass and the picture of Late President Jamal Abdul Nasir on the back. Enclosed herewith is the key of the car.

7– Your representative will find all further instructions in English in the tableau of the car opposite the front seat. He should comply with them.

7– After receiving the ransom we will directly instruct our commandoes in command of the plane to remove all arms and explosives from the plane, and to release it with its crew and passengers.

You have to move in utmost secrecy in following our instructions. The movements of your representative have to be completely secret. Any deviation from this and any attempts of any kind to inform the authorities in Germany, Lebanon and elsewhere, or any attemptto hinder in any way the procedure of delivering the ransom would result immediately in severing all contacts between us, and you will be held responsible for the results.

Let it be known that any delay in the arrival of your representative to Beirut at the exact time fixed (9.00 GMT Thursday, 24th February, 1972) will cause immediate severance of all contacts between us and consequently blowing up the plane.

Let it be also known that your representative will be under our continuous watch, control, and protection until he leaves Beirut International Airport.

This is the last you hear from us. There will be no further contact between us.

ZIONIST OCCUPATION VICTIMS ORGANISATION

Encls.
1. Table of currencies.
2. Plan of parking area.
3. Key of the car.

February 22, 3:30 P.M.: Preparations for securing the ransom money started.

A representative was chosen in case the hijackers demanded that the ransom be delivered to them directly, and a plane was chartered to take the money to Beirut.

February 22, 5:30 P.M.: A decision to agree to the hijackers' demands was made.

February 23, 12:45 A.M.: The chartered plane carrying the representative and the ransom money left for Beirut.

The Lebanese government learned of this, and the plane, when it was halfway to Beirut, was ordered to turn back.

February 23, 9:35 A.M.: A dangerous situation arose. The hijackers demanded that the hijacked plane be refueled and that food for three days be supplied. They said, "We can blow up the plane anytime. We can't wait anymore. Speed up the arrangements."

Talks were opened between Lufthansa and the Lebanese government, and the latter compromised and gave permission for the chartered plane to land in Beirut. The hijackers were informed of this, Lufthansa telling them, "We will meet your demands. A plane is on its way to Beirut to satisfy those demands."

The plane arrived in Beirut five hours and fifteen minutes later than scheduled.

The courier who delivered the ransom money later described his experience. "I followed their instructions to the letter. After passing through customs, I found an old Volkswagen as described; in it I found a precise map of the route I should take, as well as further instructions and a password. I was followed by another car as I drove about forty miles into the suburbs of Beirut after passing through three checkpoints.

"I got out at a certain point and walked a little ways. Three Arabs on a large wagon appeared very soon.

"I spoke the password and handed a trunk containing the ransom to one of the men, who checked the money. When the exchange was completed, one of the men gave me the following password: 'Our comrade, the martyr Abu Talet.' I had him write it down on a piece of paper.

"They took me back to Beirut and invited me to lunch. After the meal, they drove me to a place about four miles from the airport, where they called a taxi for me and then disappeared."

The plane was returned to Lufthansa.

None of this information was available to the Japanese government or Japan Air Lines during the period from July 20 to July 24, 1973.

And there in the letter was the unequivocable deadline, "13:00 G.M.T. on Monday 23rd July 1973," approximately eleven hours after the letter reached its destination. The threat was that the plane would be blown up unless the hijackers received instructions to the contrary. JA8109 was destroyed, but not in Dubai.

July 22

Defense Minister Rashid, still in the control tower, was excited. He had reason to be. The hijackers had demanded fuel.

"I'll say it again! Eighty thousand pounds."

"I can't give you an immediate reply."

"I give you twenty minutes. If you don't supply the fuel within twenty minutes, as I told you before, we'll blow up the plane."

"Yes, yes. But I want more time for consultations."

"That's not necessary. All you have to do is supply the fuel."

To Rashid, there was no doubt that if they were demanding fuel, they were planning to take off. It was the first time that the tension had become strained to the breaking point since the landing.

In the company of President Zaid and Prime Minister Rashid Al-Maktoum, Asada arrived at the airport. After listening to his son, the prime minister said, "Mr. Asada, I think there are three ways to solve the problem. Which one would you choose?

"The first is to give in to the hijackers' demands unconditionally.

"The second is to present some conditions of our own in order to extend the time and then come to a compromise.

"The third is to enter the plane by force and capture the hijackers.

"What do you propose? We'll cooperate with you in anything you decide."

Troops standing in the shadows of the airport buildings were ready to attack whenever the order was given. Asada felt the pressure for a decision. Kassay was adamant in his demand.

"Why are you hesitating? Give us the fuel!"

"Release the passengers first."

"Give us the fuel!"

"The passengers first!"

"So you won't listen! Then I won't speak to you until after the twenty minutes have passed."

"Wait! I'm not saying I won't give you fuel. But before that, I want the passengers released. I appeal to your humanity as an Arab. With regard to the passengers, you have forgotten the spirit of Arab mercy."

"What false words! I respect Arab humanity. I won't hurt the passengers. I have struck no one. I have done nothing to merit your vilification. Hurting a human being is contrary to my spirit of humanism."

"If you release the passengers, I promise to fill the plane's tanks with fuel."

"The only thing I can do now is demand fuel. Nothing else, including release of the passengers, can be done. I have no instructions. I want you to understand that."

Kassay spoke simply and crisply. Rashid's feeling was that the plane would certainly be flown to another destination if the fuel was supplied. He challenged Kassay again.

"You used the word *release*. Isn't *liberate* the correct word?"

"Again you have said the same thing! Have we not agreed on this already? I believe *release* is the correct term."

"I know why you said 'release.' You told me the reason. But I want you to understand that I do not accept your reason. I want to discuss this with you in more detail. Promise me you'll do so."

"I can't do so now. It would be different after you've given us fuel. The twenty minutes will soon be up."

"Can't you extend the time limit a little?"

"How many minutes more do you want?"

"Only a few. Only time enough for me to think a little more."

The Dubai government placed the airport director's office at the disposal of the relief team, and the latter lost no time in turning it into a countermeasures headquarters. Conversation between the tower and the plane was relayed to this room and simultaneously translated by the Japanese who knew Arabic. A telephone circuit was kept open between this room and the countermeasures headquarters in Tokyo. Via this, Senda reported the demand for fuel. The tension spread to Tokyo.

The question was what would happen if the fuel was provided. Would the plane only fly to another airport? Or would there be a suicidal crash on Israel?

In Tokyo the consensus was to refuse the demand. But a shockwave went through the operations center when Senda reported a four-minute deadline. He ended his report by asking, "Don't you think we should supply the fuel and then renew negotiations?" Tokyo could not reply immediately.

Oddly enough, Kassay was in a cheerful mood. If anyone in the control tower had seen him at that moment, he undoubtedly would have fallen on him with flaying fists. Despite the strain of his verbal battle with Rashid, Kassay was enjoying a cup of ice water as he turned to Konuma and asked, "Which tank should be filled?"

"The number two tank," Konuma replied without hesitation.

"Will they understand?"

"Tell them its on the right side."

"All right."

As a matter of fact, the refueling had been proposed by Konuma in the first place, because the air conditioning had been in full operation since the landing, and fuel was running low. When the chief pilot informed Kassay of this, the latter had asked how much fuel was needed. Konuma had an idea and decided to take a chance. If a large amount of fuel was pumped into only one tank, the plane would be unable to take off due to the imbalance. (Aside from this, the ten thousand pounds of fuel left in the four main tanks would have been enough for a short flight.) Konuma hoped the hijacker would not see through his plan.

"Eighty thousand pounds," he said.

"Eighty thousand pounds in number two tank. Is that correct?"

What put Rashid, Asada and the countermeasures headquarters in a tight spot was that Kassay did not pass on the information as to why he wanted the fuel, nor did he indicate that it was Konuma's idea.

As chief pilot, Konuma was the angriest person on board, but he was not quick-tempered, nor did he resort to any rash actions. Though he hated the hijackers, he concealed his anger and waited for an opportunity to turn the tables. From observing his actions closely, he had the strong feeling that Kassay was planning to stay in Dubai for a while. Moreover, he thought that it was about time a relief team arrived from Japan.

By asking that the number two tank be filled, he was actually sending out a signal. JAL flight personnel knew as a matter of course that the number two tank was connected only to the engine used for air conditioning; thus they would also know that the plane was not going to leave the airport.

Kassay's time limit was already over. Asada, pressed for a decision, chose to supply the fuel. Attacking the plane was clearly untenable, because of the passengers. It was not, after all, a military plane. But he found himself unable to surrender unconditionally. Rashid had reached the same conclusion.

As he watched the refueling operation, Asada suddenly took notice of which tank was being filled. He sent for Shun'ichi Yamaguchi, a section chief in charge of flight maintenance, who gave immediate confirmation: "There's no doubt about it. It's only AP fuel for air conditioning. They plan to stay quite a while in Dubai."

Konuma's strategy had succeeded, and when Tokyo had been informed that the refueling was completed, there was a sigh of relief. But no one imagined that it was the chief pilot's idea. In both Dubai and Tokyo, there was astonishment at the hijackers' knowledgeability and even rumors that there was a pilot among them. Nor did the story end there; the next morning, the rumors were repeated in the newspapers. (There had been a pilot among the Lufthansa hijackers.)

Meanwhile, the passengers had finished their breakfast of eggs, bread and tea. No one left his food uneaten; it was their only enjoyment.

They had not been informed where they were, but from the hot air that rushed in when food was delivered, they did know they were in the tropics. Those who raised a window shade when they dared saw only the expanse of desert and decided they were in an Arab country. Kazuhiko Matsuo assumed he was in "Dubai" from seeing the word printed on a breakfast napkin. But he did not know where the country was. None of the passengers did.

Yoshitarō Koga, a hardware merchant, was on his first trip abroad. He had had the feeling that his plane might be hijacked, because there were numerous other incidents. When it actually happened, he felt fairly resigned to his fate. But for a fifty-two-year-old man to remain seated with no information from the outside was a cause of great uneasiness. Like the others, he was used to a veritable flood of information; to be without it was almost unbearable. "What is the government doing? What is JAL doing?" He was irritated and his nerves were badly frayed.

After breakfast, trouble occurred. Returning to his seat from the toilet, one man found that he had missed his cigarette ration. It was the man who had sneaked a carton of Kents under his seat when cigarettes had been confiscated. Despite the shortage, he had not once shared his hidden treasure.

Everyone could hear him shouting that he was being discriminated against, but no one made a move to help him. Nor did anyone inform the hijackers. Not satisfied, he called a stewardess and ordered her to get his ration. When she returned empty-handed and shaking her head, he began berating her. Finally, a man one row ahead turned and handed him two of the five cigarettes he had received. With this, the man's anger subsided.

A little later, when Maruoka brought the man his ration of five cigarettes, he thanked the hijacker and shook hands with him. But he did not return the two cigarettes he had received.

The sight of Naoko was a great comfort, perhaps the only one, to the other passengers. Shouting "Hands up!" she would raise the front paws of her panda doll.

This seemed to amuse Akbal. He laughed, walked over to her and gave her some candy. She said "thank you" very clearly but placed the candy on the table without looking at the hijacker. As he walked away, her shrill voice rang out, "Hands up!" When he stopped, as if stabbed in the back, and raised his hands, a ripple of laughter ran through the compartment–for the first time.

Aware of the passengers' tenseness, Konuma felt that he should do something to relax the atmosphere. At the same time, he thought the best thing to do was to wait patiently for rescue. He did not want to provoke any incidents.

Kassay, it must be said, was treating Konuma with deference, just as he was treating Rashid. But Konuma noticed that Kassay was now in an impatient mood. He did not know the reason, nor did anyone else. He was afraid that Kassay might do something rash but continued to hope that the hijackers would recover their humanistic feelings. To realize this hope, he thought it best to treat them not as criminals but as fellow human beings. Interestingly enough, Rashid was of the same opinion, though there had been absolutely no contact between the two.

Konuma gave the following order to his crew: "Perform your duties as usual. Don't excite the hijackers by discriminating between them and the passengers. Smile to both the passengers and the hijackers."

Rashid was famous in Arab countries as a "sheikh among sheikhs" because of his great courage and refinement. Hayes had come to the conclusion that Kassay, though he did not know his name, was a cultured man. "The man who is carrying on talks with Rashid," he thought, "must be a man of refinement. In the first place, he speaks in a courteous way. Furthermore, the Arabic he uses is of a high level. He must be as highly educated as Rashid." This turned out to be true. Information from Beirut indicated that Kassay had studied politics and literature at Cairo University.

While Kassay's Arabic was of a high level, spoken mainly in cities, Rashid spoke in the local dialect. (The difference would be comparable to that between the Tokyo dialect and the dialect of northern Japan, that is, greater than the difference between any two dialects in the United States.) In an argument between a person speaking a standard dialect and one speaking a local dialect, it is usual for the former to predominate. This is true of Arabic as well, and Rashid sometimes found himself pushed into a corner.

Sitting beside Rashid was a middle-aged Englishman, who when the United Arab Emirates had become independent, stayed on as the director general of the country's security police force. When Rashid was stuck for words, the Englishman took over. He had assisted the defense minister often, and they made a good team. Their timing was perfect.

Kassay, however, did not show any signs of looking down on Rashid, though he still did not know his identity.

Their conversation resumed.

"Release the passengers."

"Why do you repeat that? I do not have the authority. I can only follow instructions. Can't you understand that?"

"I also am a soldier, so I can understand that. But I am not appealing to you as soldier to soldier. I appeal to your humanity, which every human being has naturally. Release the passengers, I'm appealing to your conscience."

"We won't harm or kill any passengers. Please believe us."

"If that's your feeling, why don't you release them? Have you no human feeling?"

Growing excited, Kassay shouted, "We are Palestinian commandos, commandos, commandos!"

"Release the passengers. If you can't free all of them, then the women and children. This is an order!"

"The only one who can give me orders is my organization."

"Don't forget that you are in the territory of the United Arab Emirates. And remember, you are not welcome here. Release the passengers!"

"Everyone aboard the plane is well. No one has been hurt. No one has become ill. This is due to the kindness accorded us by the United Arab Emirates. On behalf of my comrades, I would like to thank the president of your country. We are treating the passengers humanely. Please understand that."

"Isn't releasing the passengers humane?"

"I'm a commando."

The midday meal consisted of *suzume-zushi* and an apple. Seeing the *sushi*, Kazuhiko Matsuo knew that a relief team had arrived from Japan. He was elated. He felt that it would not be long before they were rescued. He thought of Hikoya Yamada, his boyhood friend, who worked for the weekly magazine *Shukan Shinchō*. He knew that if he could return to Japan, Yamada would be eager to hear of his experience as a hostage.

Recognizing the significance of the *sushi*, Konuma glanced at

Osamu Takagi, the copilot, and both pairs of eyes came to rest on the Japanese food.

At 3:45 that afternoon, Asada and Senda met with Rashid for their first formal talks, hoping to establish a basis for the negotiations yet to come. Rashid had been in the control tower continually for more than thirty-three hours, and his conversations with Kassay had not always been limited to the matter at hand. At times, he would quote from the Koran or argue hotly with the hijacker.

As an Arab, he was fully aware of the sufferings of the people of Palestine, whose homeland had become the state of Israel. The Palestinians were without a country, homeless and jobless. Even getting enough to eat was a problem. He could understand why the commandos were in a fighting mood, for he himself was a young sheikh in whose veins flowed the blood of the Bedouin. Nevertheless, he could not condone the acts of the terrorists. The victims were Japanese who had no connection at all with Israel. In a word, they were innocent.

Despite the absence of diplomatic ties, there had been economic exchanges ever since his country became independent, and several Japanese had contributed to the economic development of Dubai. Rashid was proud of his country and his sheikdom and believed that it was his mission to ensure the safety of the captives and ultimately to obtain their release.

As he kept watch the previous night, he had slept hardly at all. The strain showed in his face, which was pale. But he hid his exhaustion under a smile as he spoke with Asada. "Could you please tell me what you want me to do?"

At first Asada had been astonished at the defense minister's age. But watching as he talked with Kassay that morning, the doubts that he had harbored about the young sheikh's capabilities had been allayed.

Asada replied, "I thank Your Excellency for all you are doing for us. My request is that the passengers be released. If that is impossible, then I would like all the women and children to be freed immediately. If the hijackers agree to this, JAL will do all in its power to meet their demands–any demands. Please inform them of our request."

Rashid's voice was heavy. "I still can't grasp their intentions. They have made no demands. All they are doing is staying in Dubai, indefinitely it seems. My plan is to learn the name of their organization and negotiate directly with their leaders."

Asada could request nothing more. He then gave Rashid a list he had made up before leaving Tokyo. On it were the names of aged passengers and the condition of their health.

"Good," said Rashid. "I'll ask that the persons listed be freed. I'll also ask about the condition of their health at present, and if necessary, supply them with medicine."

He switched on the microphone. "Mount Carmel, this is the tower. Can you hear me?"

"Yes, this is Carmel. I hear you well. What do you want?"

"I'd like to send a mechanic to take away the GPU [air conditioning power source car]."

"All right."

"When it's been recharged, we'll send it back."

"All right. . . . Wait! A helicopter has taken off from the terminal building. Where is it going?"

"It has nothing to do with you."

"Wait a while. We'll have to check. . . . All right. Please recharge the GPU."

Talks were interrupted and resumed at 5:39.

"Could you answer my question? It's about you," asked Rashid.

"Ask anything you like."

"Please tell me the name of the organization you belong to."

"Are you trying to cross-examine me?"

"No, this is not a cross-examination. It's only a question."

"What's the Zebra time now?"

"It's 1:30 P.M. The time difference is four hours."

"I'll give you the name of our organization. We belong to the Sons of Occupied Territory Organizations. Japan's Red Army faction is a member of our organization."

"Hold on. A phone call has come for you from the outside."

"What's the man saying?"

"He says he is 'greenbelt.' Do you know who he is?"

"No, I do not."

"Do you want to listen to him?"

"No, it's not necessary. If you want to, please listen to what he has to say."

"He says that a small jet plane will take off from near the terminal building."

"Let it take off. Don't let it approach us."

About three hours earlier, JAL's Paris office had received a threatening phone call. The message was, "If you want us to release the passengers, prepare and hand over 20 million French francs." This was sent to Tokyo and from there to Dubai. When Asada asked Rashid to see if it had any connection with the hijackers, Kassay's reply was, "No, it's probably a call from a thief. Cut off his right hand."

"That's what I want to do," said Rashid. "It seems that we have reached agreement for the first time." The terrorist did not reply.

The Paris office received another threatening call two days later, and three days later, a letter demanding ransom money. On August 1, Paris police arrested the sender of the letter, a night watchman by the name of Louis Ducroix, who had no connection with the Palestinian guerrillas. He was detained to be examined by a psychiatrist.

There were a great number of people in the world like Ducroix who maintained that they had information. One man telephoned JAL's head office. All messages were relayed to Rashid, and each time he had to ask Kassay whether he had any connection with the caller. No matter how absurd they seemed, none could be ignored. When the calls were from Japan to Dubai, tension filled the air in the control tower.

"The Sons of Occupied Territory Organizations" was not a group that the defense minister had ever heard of. Basically, the guerrillas are terrorist groups organized by Palestinian Arabs, and their aim, of course, is to regain their lost land, by violence if necessary. In principle, they are under the Palestine Liberation Organization (PLO), which is a miniature state with a central committee and a parliament, as well as an army. All Arab states recognize the PLO to some extent and lend financial assistance, one country to the extent of 30 million dollars annually.

In Japan the word *guerrilla* has connotations both good and bad; in the Arab countries some rulers, for example the late King Faisal of Saudi Arabia, call the guerrillas "Fedayeen," which means guerrilla but comes from a word meaning "martyr." The guerrillas are often ready to give their lives in a jihad, or holy war.

In the long years of dispute since the founding of Israel in 1948, the ties between the PLO and the organizations under it have become increasingly complex. While they have a common objective, the two main factions within the PLO advocate different means: Al Fatah (Palestine liberation movement) is for a political settlement, but the People's Front for the Liberation of Palestine (PFLP) believes in direct action. There are also smaller groups, such as the Democratic People's Front for the Liberation of Palestine, the Palestine Liberation Force (backed by Iraq), Al Saika (backed by Syria) and others.

These organizations register with the PLO and send a representative to the PLO's national congress. There are also countless smaller groups, even ad hoc ones that disband after carrying out a particular mission. A group may lend commandos to another group for a specific action; some commandos are like militiamen, holding permanent jobs and participating only when called upon.

Among my acquaintances is a weekly magazine reporter, still in her twenties and quite attractive. We will call her *M*. In July, 1974, she met a young Palestinian while flying from Cairo to Beirut, and he invited her to his home to meet his parents and brothers.

The reason he invited her was that he wanted someone to console his parents in their grief, for his older brother had died two weeks previously in a skirmish between Israeli forces and guerrillas. *M* stayed for three days and was then invited by the youth to his apartment in Beirut, where several Palestinians, male and female, were living together. All of them had been trained at a Soviet guerrilla school and had participated in attacks against Israel.

At a camp on the outskirts of Beirut, she saw how miserable the lives of the refugees were, but she also noticed the high regard accorded the commandos. When they bid each other farewell, the young commando told *M*, "I'm leaving shortly for Kuwait, where I've found a job. But whenever the organization needs me, I'll return to do battle."

All sorts of men and women are found among the guerrillas, and their sense of unity is strong. Some do not belong to any organization. Numbers are difficult to ascertain, and even the PLO does not know how many unattached commandos there are.

Rashid was baffled by Kassay's "waiting for instructions." Contacting the PLO and the PFLP to find out about the Sons of Occupied Territory Organizations revealed nothing. No such organization was registered with the PLO, nor could it be found among the lower echelon radical groups.

In Beirut, the most Westernized of Arab cities, guerrilla organizations have established their offices openly. JAL staff from the

Arab countries and Europe had gathered at the Japanese embassy and were conferring with Ambassador Jirō Inakawa and his staff. Hoping to learn the hijackers' true objectives, the embassy was approaching the guerrilla organizations.

Ambassador Ishikawa, called back from Japan, arrived in Dubai at 5:30 P.M., by way of Kuwait. He went directly to join Asada at the countermeasures headquarters, but the person who was most happy to see him was First Secretary Kimura, who had for some reason felt embarrassed by the late arrival of his superior.

Human patience begins to weaken after a time, and when it does, outward appearances disappear and true character is revealed. The passengers had been held captive for two days, their movements greatly restricted. In the front row of the compartment, a middle-aged woman began talking to the young man next to her.

"Just look at the attitude that stewardess is taking, always smiling at the hijackers. Where does she think she is? The passengers she ignores, but when there is a young man, even a hijacker, she always smiles. Are you a bachelor? When you choose a wife, be careful not to select a girl like that one."

Whether the woman was being malicious I do not know, but before writing this book, I interviewed dozens of passengers. None of them said that the ten stewardesses ignored them and were friendly only to their captors, as the woman claimed. As a matter of fact it was quite the opposite. In order not to excite the hijackers, the girls had, of course, worn a "professional" smile whenever they came in contact with them.

This woman was probably in her forties and dressed in rather loud Western clothes. She seemed to have made a round of the fashion houses in Europe. Many of the male passengers frowned at her remarks, but she continued. "If I had a mind to, I could seduce those young men anytime. Shall I do it to kill time? In Japan, I was quite popular with young men, you know."

She chattered on without interruption. When a hijacker approached, she would stop suddenly, then start again as soon as he had passed. The opposite sex was her favorite topic, and her remarks sometimes verged on the indecent. When others tried to caution her, she glared at them.

Some male passengers apparently tried to curry favor with their captors, smiling at them and complimenting them in English. Professor Shōda was not one of them. He closed his eyes, and scarcely moving in his seat, waited patiently for new developments. It was fortunate that no one knew who he was.

Naoko, evidently tired of playing with her doll, sat in her seat and looked around absent-mindedly, her short legs dangling.

The toilet was almost overflowing.

"Could you please clean out the toilet? We'll let only one man on board."

"Wait a minute. . . . They say at least four men are necessary to clean out the toilet."

"Four aren't necessary. Two would be enough. This is not my personal opinion. The crew says so."

"The job won't be completed before the sun sets. Four persons are necessary."

"Three."

"All right, we'll send three."

One of the three was a police officer.

"Do you want any food before it gets dark?"

"At 7:30 we would like to have some sandwiches."

"All right."

"How is the chief purser?"

"He had recovered somewhat this morning, but we haven't had a report since then. Shall we check and inform you?"

"Please do that."

"Is there anything else you want?"

"There's a child on the plane. Could you bring us some milk?"

"Yes, of course."

"Please don't forget tea. We didn't have tea for lunch."

"I'm sorry. I won't let that happen again. Let's talk again after you've finished your meal. Could you set a time?"

"How is 8 o'clock? I'll want to thank you for dinner then."

"That's fine. I hope you enjoy your meal."

Their conversation was resumed at 8:13; at the time agreed on Kassay had not yet finished his evening meal. He was always the last one to eat, while the other hijackers allowed the hostages to eat before they themselves did.

This was not unusual. The same pattern had occurred in other hijackings. There had been cases where the number of meals was less than the number of passengers and also cases where there were meals for the passengers but none for the hijackers, which was obviously done intentionally.

One reason for allowing their hostages to eat first was that they did not want to see them go hungry. The passengers were undoubtedly resentful, and it would seem that an effort was being made not to anger them further. In some incidents when the number of meals was insufficient, meals were shared. This did not happen in Dubai, but it did in the KLM hijack that occurred three months later.

Another reason was that the hijackers were afraid that food and drinks might contain sedatives. By allowing the passengers to eat first, they were having the food tested.

"How was your meal?" asked Rashid.

"The sandwich was better than the *sushi*."

"I wanted to say something before we brought you your meal, but I put it off so as not to delay your meal. Now that you have finished, I'd like to ask you to release the passengers."

"If you had said that before I ate, I'm sure it would have been the worst meal in my life."

"Tell me what you are thinking right now."

"I've told you repeatedly that we're waiting for instructions. We're soldiers who follow orders."

"I'm not requesting you to free all of them. You, as a soldier, can tell which ones should be released. Couldn't you at least free all aged persons, women and children?"

"I can't do that."

"Are you afraid of having only strong men remain on board?"

"Don't speak so crudely! I won't get angry because I know your intention is to provoke me. I'm a brave commando."

"It's not mere provocation. My feeling is that you are afraid of such a situation."

"If you say that again, I'll blow up the plane. I have the authority, you know."

"I can't promise not to do so. I'm not in a mood to make that promise. I know that Palestinian guerrillas are willing to die with the passengers. But I'd like to repeat. Please free all women and children. Immediately!"

"I can't do that."

"All right, then. This is an order from the United Arab Emirates. Release the four-year-old girl and her mother now."

"I can't obey that order."

"You're insulting the United Arab Emirates. As a citizen of this country, I cannot condone your action."

"I have no intention of insulting your country. I've prepared a message of gratitude to His Excellency the President. Afterwards, I'll kneel down in apology. But I want you to understand the position I'm in at present. I'm a commando . . ."

"Don't you feel any mercy toward children? If you're a real Arab, you can't possibly hold children captive with grown men. Are you really an Arab? Are you a human being in whose veins flows Arab blood?"

"You're suspicious not only of my heart but of my fatherland. I am, like you, a pure Arab."

"I'll ask you again. Are you really an Arab who believes in the merciful and omnipresent Allah?"

"I believe in the merciful and omnipresent Allah more than anyone else. The teachings of the Koran overflow my blood."

"I'd like to believe that. But I can't."

"You're now trying to insult me with unthinking words."

"No. I'm only suspicious of your humaneness."

"I've already clarified your suspicions. I'm a Palestinian commando!"

"That proves nothing. A soldier who believes in Allah is a courageous and merciful soldier. You have no mercy. All you can do is depend on instructions. You do not have the courage to free children on your own judgment. You're a coward!"

"No! I'm a soldier–a soldier who obeys orders faithfully."

"I also am a soldier. But I'm not a cowardly soldier who calmly sits and watches the sufferings of women and children. Free the child at least, and I'll believe that you are a real soldier of Allah."

"That I can't do."

"You're a coward! A soldier without courage. You're not an Arab!"

"No, no! I'm a brave soldier. I'm an Arab and a Palestinian."

"You're only a cowardly soldier! You're a coward!"

"No, no, no, I'm not a coward!"

Their excitement reached such a pitch that they lapsed into silence briefly. Then Kassay changed the subject.

"The ramp used when meals are brought is still resting against the side of the plane. Have it removed."

"The release of the passengers comes first. At least let the child and her mother use the ramp."

"I've never talked with one so obstinate as you. Let me speak to the man in charge of the airport. I want to have formal talks with him–not you. Call him please."

Rashid made no response.

"Can you hear me? I don't want to talk with you. I want to talk with the airport director."

"I'm in charge of the airport. I'm Rashid. I'm the defense minister."

Kassay was astounded. After a slight pause, his voice took on a different tone.

"No, you're not. Your voice is different."

"No, the voice is mine. I'm Rashid."

"Are you really the defense minister?"

"That's right."

"The sheikh! Is it really the sheikh?"

"Yes . . . Now let's have formal talks. You want to, don't you?"

"Yes, I'll tell you again. We're Arabs; we're citizens of Palestine. We're representatives of the citizens of Palestine. We're human beings. Mr. Defense Minister, if you have anything to ask us, feel free to do so."

Up to that moment, Kassay had not known that he was speaking to the sheikh. His style of speech, as I mentioned before, was that of an educated man. It now became even more polite.

"I ask you as an official representative of my government. Are you going to leave this airport peacefully? Or do you want to stay here longer?"

"We stay . . . until we receive instructions. We won't harm the passengers or cause damage to the plane."

"The United Arab Emirates requests the 'Sons of Occupied Territories' and the Red Army faction to release women and children."

"I understand how you feel. But I can't go against orders. We have done nothing to the passengers. Please respect our instructions."

"I see. I'll respect your wishes. But if we negotiate directly with your organization, would you free the women and children?"

"I don't know. I can say that our leaders are in occupied territory [Israel], and instructions will come to us through you. Our answer will also be relayed through you."

"We have received many messages since this morning requesting us to send greetings to the commandos on the plane. Among them are some that seem to have been sent from very near the airport. I do not know which ones have come from your organization."

"Our organization is an international–not a local–one."

"I understand that. All I can do now is pray for the health of the passengers, crew and yourselves."

"I haven't heard such kind words from you before. I'd like to thank you for being so considerate to us."

"I'm happy to hear that."

"Please remove the ramp. I can't sleep well with it there."

"It will be done."

Communication ended for the day. The time was 10:45. The defense minister remained where he was. Asada, leaving the control tower, was met by fifty reporters and cameramen.

A Tense Atmosphere

From Abu Dhabi to Dubai a single paved road runs straight through the desert. An official of the United Arab Emirates had met me at the airport, but I spent only a few minutes talking with him before getting into the car that was waiting.

The speedometer needle pointed steadily at seventy miles per hour, no more, no less. It had been excruciatingly hot at the airport, and even in the car the heat was enervating. There was no other traffic as we headed directly toward the heat waves shimmering on the horizon. Parallel to the road ran a reddish brown oil pipeline; between it and the road the corpses of camels were piled here and there. I found it disconcerting to repeatedly see the bleached white bones.

The city of Dubai appeared suddenly, like a mirage.

At the Carlton International Hotel, I signed the register, writing my name in Chinese characters and underneath that "Satō Bunsei" in Roman letters. But I soon wondered why I had done that. On all my previous trips overseas, I had invariably signed it "Bunsei Satō," following the Western style. Was I, I wonder, thinking subconsciously of my role as a representative of the government? At the time I wondered if it might not be my last signature.

That was not the only strange thing I did. I took my suitcase to my room and left it there unopened. As I was closing the door on my way out, I thought, "What will happen to my suitcase if I become a hostage?" As I look back on that day, I question why strange thoughts entered my head; it must have been due to the tension. (I am reminded of a friend of mine whose house caught fire. He entered the burning house and took away only one thing–his pillow.)

I left immediately for the airport.

While I was crossing the desert, the passengers were finishing their breakfast of bread, eggs, cake, fruit, milk and water, which they had been ordered to eat as quickly as possible. Since being awakened at 4:20 that morning, the treatment they had been receiving had been harsh. They had soon been made to hold up their hands for twenty minutes.

This stimulated them, because they felt that something was in the air on this, the third day of their captivity. The excited way in which the orders were issued contributed to this impression.

Not all of the passengers were perceptive. One man, who had always smiled and tried to strike up a conversation when one of the terrorists passed by, raised his hands only slightly. He did this again when one of them passed, but the hijacker shouted, "Higher!" Chastened, he raised his hands higher. After that, instead of trying to be friendly, he turned his face away when approached.

The woman who had expressed her willingness, and ability, to seduce her captors did not obey the order. Even when one of them rushed up and repeated the order, she did not comply. After being threatened with a grenade, she reluctantly held up her hands, but as he walked away, she muttered, "What is this? Snarling at us at this hour of the morning?" Evidently she was heard, for he came back and without a word slapped her face. She became silent.

Naoko was awakened with the others and put up her hands. Soon they came down. She was asleep again. None of the hijackers said anything, but a middle-aged woman was heard to say, "I wish I were a child too!" No one heard only envy in the words; they were more sarcastic than envious.

Chief pilot Konuma felt that something was going to happen that day. Maybe he would have to fly someplace. He made up his mind to rest as much as possible, to prepare himself physically and mentally.

By this time the hijackers were very excited. They ran back and forth, shouting at their hostages. In particular the bearded Akbal and the tall Peralta spoke loudly and watched intently to see that orders were obeyed. Again and again, Peralta climbed the circular stairs to the upper deck, entered the cockpit and surveyed the airport. Then he returned to the compartment and paced back and forth. Akbal, on the other hand, strode up and down the aisles, glaring at the passengers.

Maruoka appeared to be nervous, because whenever he paced the aisles, he kept his eyes on the floor and avoided the eyes of the passengers. Still, at times, he shouted and scolded. Of the four, he seemed to be the most emotionally unstable.

Forty minutes ahead of schedule, at 7:20 A.M., Kassay suddenly contacted the tower.

"A fire engine is approaching again. What are your intentions?"

"It's an ordinary morning routine."

"Why didn't you inform me beforehand? If you do it again, I'll blow up the plane. Do you understand?"

"Yes. It'll never happen again."

Ten minutes later, "We'd like to have breakfast."

"We're preparing it."

"We want breakfast now."

"We'll bring the meals as soon as they're ready. Breakfast yesterday was at 8:30."

"I want it brought as soon as possible."

"Okay."

"Can you tell me how much longer it will take you?"

"I'll check."

"Please do so."

Rashid, listening to the conversation between Kassay and the operator, knew from the sound of the voice that the former was excited. Like those on the plane, he felt something was in the air.

Besides Rashid, there were in the tower five air controllers, ten soldiers and two policemen. The room, however, was not very large, and much of the space was taken up by equipment. Just then, Asada, Senda, Gotō, Ambassador Ishikawa and other members of the relief team came up the stairs from the elevator.

Rashid wore a stern expression. He had slept little during his two days and two nights in the control tower. He was pale; he looked tired. Moreover, his tenseness was heightened by the tone of Kassay's voice. The room was full to overflowing, but he spoke softly, "Could the Japanese side limit the number of staff members entering this room?" Only Asada and four or five others were allowed to remain.

Preparatory to delivering breakfast, a ramp was placed at the front door of the plane at ten minutes past eight. Ten minutes later, Kassay said, "Please bring our breakfast."

"It's now being loaded on a truck."

"Hurry, please."

"Yes, yes."

Breakfast was delivered at 8:30.

Ten minutes later, Kassay wanted to know if the airport was closed.

"Yes, it's been closed because of you. Is there anything you want to know about the closure?"

"No."

The passengers were ordered to finish their breakfast quickly, and as they finished, the order was, "Hands up!"

If the instructions in the blackmail letter had been followed, Red Army activists Matsuda and Matsuura would have been on "(BA)

Flight No 765 departing Bombay. . ." It is to be assumed that the flight, due in Dubai at 8:20 A.M., would have been allowed to land. I do not know the extent of Kassay's knowledge about the hijacking plan, but judging from his frantic activity on the morning of July 23, he must have been expecting the arrival of the two activists. There is no doubt that he did not know that the letter had gone astray and was at that very moment being scrutinized by JAL officials and the police in Tokyo.

It was already afternoon in Tokyo when Shigeo Yamada walked into the countermeasures headquarters at the airport. He had passed several reporters, who did not know who he was, nor did they know what he carried. If they had, they would surely have stopped and questioned him.

As he entered the room, Yūichirō Hagihara, chief of the information section at the head office, stared at him in amazement. What was Yamada doing here? After all, though he had been the first Japanese to be involved in a hijack, his present position was manager of the Tokyo branch office. (Meanwhile, at the Pacific Hotel in Shinagawa, family members were importuning the airline to take them immediately to Dubai.)

In a sense, Yamada himself did not know what he was carrying. He had been working in his office that morning as usual, but when he went through the ordinary mail delivered to his desk around 11 o'clock, he became the first person to read the blackmail letter. He could not believe his eyes.

As he sped down the expressway to the airport, he was in a state of great agitation. Was the letter real? Was it fake? Had it been sent by the terrorists? Or by somebody else? Why had it been delayed?

He knew about the Lufthansa hijack the preceding year and the demand for 5 million dollars. He had the feeling that the guerrillas might belong to the same organization. But there was no solid evidence, and he kept his thoughts to himself. There were others who thought as Yamada did but also kept silent. At that time, news reports were the only information in Japan about the earlier hijacking. However, I believe that Yamada and the others were correct. A comparison of the two letters leaves little doubt that they were from the same source.

Various officials, including Vice President Takagi, were waiting for Yamada's arrival. They did not know whether the letter was real or not, but if it was, it was the first word from the hijackers. Yamada supervised the translation into Japanese, and as they conferred over a copy of the translation, they spoke in quiet tones. The deadlines set in the letter had already passed, except for one. The question was what to do next.

Threatening letters and phone calls had been an added burden to the airline and had, in fact, kept staff members quite busy. One man showed up at the head office and offered to handle the negotiations.

Midmorning, 10 A.M.

"Mount Carmel, can you hear me? This is tower."

"Yes, I can hear you well. Do you have something to tell me?"

"A team representing Japan Air Lines has arrived. JAL President Asada wants to speak with the Japanese Red Army faction commando in Japanese. Is this possible?"

"Absolutely not. We won't speak in Japanese. Also, we will not talk to a Japanese company. As I said before, we can only talk to the government of Dubai."

Asada did not give up. With Hideo Kyōno as his interpreter, he tried valiantly to open up direct discussions with the terrorists.

Rashid took over the microphone from the controller.

"Good morning. This is Defense Minister Muhammed Rashid. How are you feeling?"

"Good morning, Your Excellency. I'm feeling fine. The passengers and we are all fine, physically and mentally, thanks to the kindness of Your Excellency, the people of Dubai and the officials of the United Arab Emirates. I'd like to thank you for your kindness. Your Excellency, have you been here since this morning?"

"I've been here since you arrived. I've been watching over the safety of you and the passengers."

"I'm very grateful. Your Excellency, do you have anything to tell me?"

"Yes, Will you talk with President Asada of JAL? He was here last night until you went to bed. He got up early this morning and is here now. He wants to speak to you."

"I'm sorry, Your Excellency, but I hope you understand the position I'm in. I haven't received instructions."

"I see."

"A fire engine approached us this morning. We're worried that explosives might have been placed on the fire engine."

"You don't have to worry. Aren't we both Arabs? I don't do cowardly things. I have no intention of attacking you."

"I'm glad to hear such words."

"Here's a message for you. In the name of the United Arab Emirates and its citizens, I demand the release of the passengers. Three nights have passed. If you're waiting for instructions from your superiors, I'd like to contact them in your place. I'd also like to contact any of your representatives."

"I'd like you to do so if it were possible. But it's not. As freedom fighters and soldiers of the Red Army faction, we'd like to request that Your Excellency and the president wait a little while longer."

"We ask you to let us make contact with your organization."

"I know how you feel. I'll tell Your Excellency one thing, on my own initiative. It won't be long before we receive instructions."

"Your words have reached my ears."

As soon as I reached the airport, I conferred with Asada. He told me about his attempts to speak to the Japanese hijacker and the hijackers refusal to talk with anyone except the Dubai government or in any language except Arabic.

"Is that what Defense Minister Rashid said?" I asked.

"No, not exactly him. The reply came from a man who said he was the information officer. He's the assistant chief of police."

"Then you haven't been able to talk with the hijackers?"

"No. In the first place it was only a little while ago that our arrival was made known to them." I sympathized with him, wondering what was the use of coming all the way from Japan if the terrorists refused to talk with us.

I had received no prior information about Rashid. I thought his efforts to obtain the release of the passengers were worthy of the highest respect, and I was astonished to learn that he had not once come down from the control tower. I thought that a politician should follow his example.

Still, Rashid was not listening to Asada's opinion; he seemed intent on solving the incident in his own way. I began to think that he was arrogant.

"What strategy is the defense minister taking?" I asked.

"We were given three options: meet all their demands, place some conditions on meeting their demands, or carry out an armed attack. Needless to say, I told them that the third was no option at all. I advised them that we favored the second method."

"That was the best choice," I agreed.

"But not one passenger has been released, although all their demands for food, water and other daily necessities have been met."

"What's the relationship between the hijackers and Dubai?"

"The hijackers seem to be Arabs, just as the people here are."

"In any case, let's advise Rashid in the strongest terms that we're willing to listen to all demands, including the payment of ransom money, to obtain the release of the hostages." It was becoming obvious that the Japanese government could not solve the incident by itself, in its own way. Clearly, it could no longer be assumed that the situation had any similarity to the hijacking of the Yodo-go.

While I was receiving reports from Asada, Senda and Ambassador Ishikawa, the switchboard operator said, "A call to Ambassador Ishikawa from Red Army faction headquarters in Tokyo has come in. Does the ambassador wish to take the call?"

I thought that the hijacker's organization was finally making contact with us, but before replying I talked with the operations center in Tokyo and ordered them to have the call traced. To do this, of course, we had to prolong the call as much as possible.

Since he was a man used to the ways of diplomacy, I wondered if the ambassador should take on this job, but the call had come to him personally, so I asked him to take it. He was a man of integrity, with nothing to hide, but perspiration was streaming down his face even before he picked up the receiver.

The caller identified himself as a member of the Red Army faction and asked to be called "Ishihara." He seemed very self-composed, but his words seemed to mock us.

He said, "JAL appears to have 3 million dollars in surplus money that it proposes to pay as ransom to the hijackers. Don't do it! If you have such money, donate it to the PLO or another clearly known organization for the liberation of Palestine.

"Don't spend the money for any useless purpose!"

What he said was ridiculous, but since he claimed to be a member of the Red Army faction, we could not cut the call short. Suspicious that there might be a hidden meaning, the ambassador tried valiantly to find it. By this time he was drenched with perspiration. The caller hung up abruptly after a final word, "Pass on what I have said to President Asada." The conversation lasted three minutes and forty seconds.

Ridiculous as it was, we began to suspect that the hint was to pay the ransom money to the PLO or PFLP. The call bothered me, but soon after that the report on the blackmail letter came in, and we began to believe that the letter had more substance than the call.

After the incident had been settled, a man came to JAL's head office and in a loud voice asserted that the method of settling the incident had been "atrocious." He was arrested and under questioning confessed that he had made the call. He was not a member of the Red Army faction. Reading in the newspaper that JAL was about to pay ransom money, he had called in a fit of anger. He must have been in a state of frenzy during the four or five hours it took for a call to go through. The man was a clerk at a primary school. I could not but wonder how such a man could continue to work at a school without causing trouble.

I set out for the control tower to talk with Rashid, and we passed a group of correspondents on the way. One of them shouted, "Mr. Vice Minister! Three days have passed. Why are you leaving everything up to the Dubai government. Can't you do anything?" He seemed quite irritated by the lack of progress. I realized that what he was saying was true and thought, "I'm going to do something about this."

Beyond the runway, there was nothing to see but the desert. The sun beat down without mercy. Turbaned soldiers were still in the shadows of the buildings, their weapons cradled in their arms. There were also armored cars, ready for action. The plane stood in solitary silence.

Kassay was trying to have chief purser Miyashita returned to him. "How is the injured man? Is he still alive? If he is, would you please give us a detailed report on the extent of his injuries?"

"He's still alive. But he hasn't recovered from the shock. These are the only two things we can tell you right now."

"Your answer is not sufficient. Please tell us in detail."

"We'll check and then inform you."

Rashid had no intention of returning the chief purser. But to keep his promise, he ordered one of his subordinates to go to the hospital. He did not forget to mention that the diagnosis should indicate that the patient's condition was graver than it actually was.

As I mentioned before, the elevator in the control tower is very small. It seemed to me that it had been a long time since I learned of the hijacking and a long time had been spent in getting to Dubai. My fighting spirit was aroused.

I felt anger against those who had opposed my giving myself up as a hostage. Now I was battling the fear of death. Going for broke is an attitude not uncommon among the Japanese. But what if the terrorists took the same attitude? To prevent them from taking suicidal action I decided I must instill in them a respect for the value of human life.

It is not easy to change the mind of a person who has decided to die. In this light, I did not think my suggestion that I take the plane to Narita airport, or fly them anywhere at all, was either absurd or fantastic. If they were in a suicidal frame of mind, it would be well worth it. In fact, any reasonable demand would be met if it preserved the lives of the terrorists and the passengers and crew. With that I felt free from the fear of death.

Rashid was another matter. He had met with the relief team only once and then briefly. I could not understand why he did not consult the Japanese side. My impression was that he was not only young but brash. I made up my mind that he should no longer continue to ignore us.

With me were Otokodake from the Civil Aviation Bureau and First Secretary Kimura, who was fluent in Arabic. The three of us filled the elevator. I asked Kimura to "interpret accurately for me, because from now on it looks as if there is going to be a struggle between Rashid and myself."

Rashid appeared even younger than I had expected. He was a handsome young man, though his sandaled feet were dusty. His turban, however, was spotlessly white. (I discovered later that he had changed it when he learned that he was to meet a representative of the Japanese government.) The fatigue was plainly visible in his wan face; his eyes shone brilliantly.

From the tower window, I looked out over the runway and the desert beyond. Not a cloud in the deep blue sky. On the distant horizon appeared a black dot. It grew larger and larger and spread out into a large troop of Bedouin horsemen–but it was my imagination, inspired by the intrepid look on Rashid's face.

First I thanked him and told him how grateful the Japanese people were, for they were watching television and listening to the radio and had come to know about his courageous efforts. I told him how much I respected him.

He seemed embarrassed but said, "I'm acting according to instructions from the president and my father, the prime minister. Although I've done all in my power to have the hostages freed, none have been released. I want to apologize to the government and people of Japan." He spoke simply, even naively, his words full of humility. As Kimura interpreted, Rashid looked straight at me and nodded each time.

In my desire to see that he was fully informed of the government's position, I said something that seemed to upset him. "The Japanese government will do anything to obtain the release of the passengers and crew. Please ask the hijackers what they demand."

He was momentarily shocked.

I continued, "If ransom money is needed, we'll pay it, no matter how enormous the amount."

This seemed to hurt his pride. He retorted, "If they demand ransom, my country will pay it."

"Why should your country pay it?"

"Because the incident occurred in Dubai."

"But the plane, the passengers are Japanese . . ."

"We're in Dubai. What has happened in Dubai must be settled by Dubai."

I was forced into silence by the lucidity of his reply and his strong national pride. But I did not want to let the matter rest there.

"Please arrange for us to talk with the hijackers. I'd like to talk with the Japanese who's among them."

"I'll try to do that." Then he explained about their previous refusals. "I'll relay your request, but I don't think it will come to anything."

On hearing this from him, I felt that my mission was futile. I pleaded with him to promise that he would do his utmost.

Finally he said, "I'll persuade the hijackers to allow you to speak to them." To himself he muttered, "I wonder what they will say."

Then he continued, "Mr. Satō, I'm concentrating my efforts on calming their excited feelings. They're soldiers and they're very tense. It's important to calm them before they do something rash. They're ready to destroy the plane at any time."

I was in agreement with this; after all, it was the same as my strategy. Then I played what I thought was my highest card.

"Tell them that I'm willing to board the plane as a hostage in place of the passengers and crew. Tell them that it would be an exchange, the same as exchanging them with my government."

Rashid's reply was negative. "I've told them repeatedly," he said, "that I'd give myself up as a hostage. Each time they said the same thing: 'no exchange passengers, no exchange aircraft, no exchange anything!' "

I was astonished. I had not imagined that Rashid would offer himself as a hostage. Why should he? (Japanese newspapers, with the advantage of hindsight, pointed out that Yamamura's strategy had worked in the Yodo-go incident because the hijackers were

Japanese and in the event they were Arab guerrillas, it would fail.)

"Why," I asked him, "did you want to give yourself as a hostage? You're not Japanese. What made you consider it?"

"Isn't it natural for me to do so when the aged, women and children on the plane are suffering so much? This is an Arab country. Anything that happens here must be settled by Arabs. To uphold the pride and respect of an Arab country, I must do it. As long as the plane is here, I'll do all in my power to free the passengers and crew. If it is flown to another Arab country, that country will no doubt do the same."

Rashid's words, reflecting not only strong national pride but a firm desire not to have domestic affairs meddled in, remain vivid in my memory. Not long after this, there occurred the Kim Dae Jung incident, in which a critic of the South Korean government was kidnapped from a Tokyo hotel and taken to Seoul. I took the attitude that he should be returned immediately since the incident occurred in Japan. Perhaps I was influenced by the defense minister's words, but it is clear that a foreign power must never intervene in the domestic affairs of another country no matter what the circumstances are.

I then explained the government's attitude toward Israel. In principle Japan's Middle East policy is neutral, I told him. For one thing, there was a joint declaration issued by former Prime Minister Eisaku Satō and the late King Faisal to the effect that Japan recognized the right of Palestine to independence. Moreover, Japan was among the first countries to vote for a UN resolution recognizing this right. And Japan's initial donation of 50 thousand dollars for the relief of Palestinian refugees had subsequently been raised to 1.8 million dollars.

Only a month earlier, Minister of International Trade and Industry Yasuhiro Nakasone had visited Arab countries on a goodwill mission. And I myself was chairman of the Liberal Democratic

Party's subcommittee on Arab countries in the party's Afro-Asian Research Council. I had participated in numerous conferences on Arab affairs and was one of the few members of the Diet who had more than a superficial understanding of Arab countries. I told Rashid all this, emphasizing that Japan's policies were aimed at fostering friendly relations.

Rashid promised to continue his efforts to persuade the guerrillas to speak with me.

On leaving the control tower, I was again surrounded by newsmen. I gave them a summary of my talks without mentioning the matter of a hostage, but one of them, quite unable to conceal his frustration, shouted at me, "Mr. Vice Minister, what are you waiting for anyway? Aren't you being twisted around the little finger of the Arabs?" It was a reporter who had accompanied me from Tokyo.

"Our strategy will be a failure if even one person is killed or injured," I replied.

My answer did not satisfy him; he continued to press me, but I had to leave it at that. He was young, and apparently he had no understanding of how different the situation was from what it would have been in Japan.

An incident occurred not long after. At 12:18, the communication from the tower was, "We'll bring your lunch to you. We'll place a ramp against the plane."

"Don't let anyone except the one who puts the ramp in position approach us."

"That's understood."

At 12:40 the operator said, "The meals are ready. Are you ready?"

"We're ready. Bring the meals."

"There'll be three men. Don't make any mistake and fire on them."

"All right. What's the temperature now?"

"It's 100 degrees."

"Thanks. After you've loaded the meals on the plane, take the ramp sixty feet away from the plane."

"Isn't that a bit strange?"

"Do as we say!"

Lunch consisted of bread, roast chicken, vegetables, soft drinks and water. After they delivered it, the three men did not take the ramp away, because they had not received word to do so from the tower.

As they moved away from the plane, the bearded one stood in the door, arms akimbo and shouting. It was the first time that any of the terrorists had allowed himself to be seen.

"Take the ramp away! Take the ramp away!" he screamed.

It seemed strange that Akbal should be so excited by such a trivial matter as the removal of the ramp. "Something is about to happen. They're planning to do something. And very soon," I thought. But even Rashid could not decipher their intentions.

Messages

The terrorists' attitude became no more relaxed during the afternoon. It was three days since the plane had taken off from Paris.

Maruoka was screaming, "Hold up your hands! Hands up! Don't look to the side! Don't look to the back! If you don't obey our orders, we'll shoot. It's different this time. Hands up!"

Shigeharu Hayashi thought that something was sure to happen. He joined his hands behind his head and with his eyes sought out his wife, who had been moved to a different part of the compartment.

In the back, a woman began to shout. It was the would-be seducer. "Why are you making us hold up our hands? I don't like it. I won't do it!"

The bearded one said nothing. He raised his fist and struck her on the back of the head. She lapsed into silence but managed to glare at the man.

Naoko, now very tired, ignored the order. As he passed by, the bearded one smiled and patted her on the head.

At 3 P.M. there was a call from the tower.

"We've received a telegram from a man who calls himself a resident of West Germany. It's for you. It says that we should hand the telegram directly to you as quickly as possible. Tell us how we may deliver it."

"You don't have to deliver it. Just read it."

"It's in English. Have someone who understands English listen to the message."

"I'll listen. Read it out loud. By the way, change the frequency."

"All right, change the frequency to 118.3 megacycles.

"I'll read the telegram: 'IF YOU TO KILL PASSENGER ON BOARD, DO SO AT ONCE, OTHERWISE BE HUMAN ENOUGH TO RELEASE THEM/IT SOUNDS RIDICULOUS IF YOU PERMIT THOSE WHO YOU OBVIOUSLY WANT TO KILL TO RECEIVE REFRESHMENT AND MEALS/PLEASE GIVE UP YOUR INTENTION/THERE ARE OTHER WAYS MEANS OF UNBLOODY POSSIBILITY TO REACH YOUR POLITICAL AIMS/SIGNED 13569 INHABITANT OF FEDERAL REPUBLIC OF GERMANY.' Shall I reread it?"

"No, it's not necessary."

"Does the message or the man have any connection with you?"

"No comment. I'm going to end our conversation here for a while."

At 3:30 Kassay called the tower. "We've got an answer to the telegram. Send it out."

"To whom shall we send it?"

"To the place where it came from."

"Tell me your answer."

"We've come up with an answer that will teach them a lesson." Rashid could hear Kassay laughing with one or another of his comrades.

"Send the message exactly as I say: 'Our answer is silence'... Can you hear me?"

"Yes. I don't know the address. Can you tell me?"

"I told you before. Send the telegram to where the other one came from."

"It will be done."

Although the message looked as if it might be the work of a deranged person, Kassay reacted differently than he had previously. He sent a reply rather than simply ignoring it. And he had said, "teach *them* a lesson." Was there any significance in the plural form?

Rashid thought that it must have been waiting for the telegram that had caused the increased tension that day and worried about what they were going to do next. He ordered that the state of readiness of the troops at the airport be checked.

As I mentioned before, the people who read the blackmail letter in Tokyo found it incredible. Yoshinori Shibata of the police agency pointed out the absurdity of one person's transporting that amount of money by himself, but this was only one factor against regarding the letter as genuine.

Neither Shibata nor Shintani nor anyone else could understand how such a crucial message could be delivered late. And why should it be sent by ordinary mail? It should be noted that in Japan one does not mail a letter, even by ordinary mail, with the expectation that delivery will be delayed; even so, a letter arriving one day late is not terribly extraordinary. Special delivery is uncomplicated and widely used. A rubber special delivery stamp and stamp pad can easily be bought at any department store or even at a neighborhood stationery store.

Why such an odd sum? The demand was for 3.998 billion. Why not simply 4 billion yen? (Fusako Shigenobu later explained that the amount was the same as that paid as solatium by the Japanese government after the Lod Airport massacre. But this seems absurd, for the money was now being demanded of Japan Air Lines, not the government. If she meant to criticize the amount of solatium, why did she not indicate that the intention was that the government should pay the ransom?) At any rate, there was nothing in the letter itself to indicate the reason for the odd sum, and Shibata particularly was wracking his brains to understand it.

Shibata also checked the airline timetables regarding the flight numbers and times given in the letter and found a number of discrepancies. Had the writer(s) misread the timetable? Or were the errors an indication of his (or their) mentality?

Various factors led Shibata to say that "if the letter is not fake, then the sender must be stupid. How can a crime, such as a hijack, which necessitates precise planning, be carried out by a dimwit?"

Only three hours remained before the time given in the letter for blowing up the plane. Before the money could be sent to Dubai, it had to be obtained–in the currencies of six different countries. As for the foreign currency, the simple fact was that such a large amount was not readily available in Japan.

After obtaining approval at a cabinet meeting, Shintani asked Minister of Finance Takeo Fukuda to help him obtain the money. The latter agreed, of course, and they finally came to the conclusion that they would have to obtain the sum (14 million dollars) in U.S. currency. The problem was how to do this.

The banks in Japan holding American dollars are the city banks, of which there are fourteen major ones. But of these only seven or eight had 1 million dollars each, and these constituted necessary reserves. Not only was the amount insufficient but even the Ministry of Finance would find it difficult to request the banks to lend it their reserves. Consequently, Vice Minister of Finance Hideyuki Aizawa and Michiya Matsukawa, director of the ministry's international finance bureau, advised Vice Minister of Transport Kōichi Takabayashi that "it is impossible to procure 14 million dollars in Japan. There is no alternative to obtaining the money in Switzerland. We'll arrange for it without delay."

Takabayashi informed Shintani, who then wished there were a Buddhist or Shinto altar in his office at which he could offer a prayer.

Although the countermeasures headquarters was a joint one–the government and the airline—various things were going on. JAL was trying to obtain 5 million dollars through the Bank of Tokyo and its overseas offices. Shibata did not know about either of these attempts to procure the ransom money. And in Dubai, though I was the government's representative, I did not know about the consultations between the Ministry of Transport and the Ministry of Finance. In fact, I did not know about it until the incident was over. Here, it seems, the inherent weakness of bureaucracies, particularly regarding communication, was in evidence.

Shibata and his subordinates continued to be skeptical about the letter, but he was worried about one particular point: "Sons of Occupied Land Organization." The first of the two postmarks indicated that the letter had been mailed between the evening of July 20 and noon of the following day. When Kassay had revealed the name of his organization as "Sons of Occupied Territory Organizations," it had been 3:29 A.M., July 23, in Japan. Therefore, the letter had been mailed some thirty-nine to fifty-five hours earlier. And while the words were not identical, the similarity in meaning was too close to be ignored.

This was a vital point in deciding to treat the letter as genuine, whether is actually was or not. Even so, Shibata and his subordinates were not entirely convinced. They still thought that demands would come from the hijackers themselves.

The Third Public Security Section faced another problem. "If JAL agrees to pay the ransom," said Shibata, "what should we do about the demand for the release of the two Red Army activists?" He did not want to release them, nor in fact could he. That matter had to be decided by the government and the public prosecutor's office, although Shibata and his men had actually made the arrests.

They did not want to take the letter at face value, but their actions were proceeding in the opposite direction.

Minister Shintani decided to handle the letter with great caution. First he would contact the hijackers for confirmation, but even if the letter were fake, he would inform them of the government's willingness to ransom the crew and passengers. He sent the contents of the letter to Dubai with the following instructions.

"1. Ask the hijackers whether the letter was sent by their organization.

"2. If reply is affirmative, point out that the letter was received at 11:45 A.M. July 23 by JAL Tokyo branch office. It was impossible for anyone from here to depart by plane from Tokyo on July 22 as demanded.

"3. The letter says that the plane would be blown up at exactly 1 P.M. GMT if we do not follow instructions. Ask whether they received such instructions from their headquarters.

"4. Because of the late delivery JAL cannot follow instructions to take the ransom money to the designated place by the designated time. Ask the hijackers for new instructions. If the reply is negative, ask whether they have intentions to free the passengers, crew and plane if we pay ransom money later than the designated time."

The time in Japan was 6:54 P.M., and in Dubai, 1:45 P.M.; in three hours it would be "13:00 G.M.T."

After reading the letter, Defense Minister Rashid said, "There's no doubt that it's bogus. I'll inform the hijackers of the letter when the opportunity arrives."

Staff members of Japanese trading firms in Lebanon were still attempting to gather information. They went through the streets of Beirut searching for any lead that would help them identify the guerrilla organization involved in the hijack. Their efforts were also intended to inform the organization of the delayed delivery of the letter and the impossibility of meeting the deadline.

In the plane, the passengers were holding up their hands; they were not permitted to go to the toilet. This went on for one hour and eight minutes before they were allowed to lower them–for five minutes. At 3:50 P.M. they were forced to raise them again.

Rashid had come to feel that the hijackers were preparing for departure. In this he was correct. Kassay was telling Konuma that he wanted the plane refueled. He wanted enough fuel to fly twenty thousand miles.

Konuma was worried. The inner panes of the lounge windows were only cracked, but at high altitudes the difference between inside and outside pressure might cause the outer panes to shatter. Flying at low altitudes would consume more fuel.

By 4:30 P.M. I was extremely worried. Only thirty minutes were left before 13:00 GMT. Rashid had still not told the hijackers about the letter.

At 4:38 the defense minister tried to find out the terrorists' real intention. He asked, "Do you want tooth brushes or underwear?"

"No, we want nothing."

"What about your evening meal?"

"We haven't thought about it. But please prepare it."

It seemed almost certain to Rashid that they were planning to take off.

A couple of minutes later, I entered the control tower. Pointing out that there was no time left, I urged Rashid to inform the hijackers of the letter. I remember vividly the look of bewilderment on his face after Kimura finished interpreting.

He looked at his watch, sprang from his chair, and quickly exchanged places with the operator who had been at the microphone. He settled into the chair. Three minutes remained before 5 P.M.

"I have an urgent message for you. Will you accept it?"

"Where did it come from?"

"Japan."

"All right. Please read it."

"The Japanese Ministry of Transport has received a letter signed 'Sons of Occupied Territory Organizations.' The letter demands the following: 1. Payment of 15 million dollars in ransom money in Aden. 2 Handing over two Japanese Red Army faction leaders currently in prison in Japan. Do you know anything about this letter?"

"We only accept instructions from our headquarters! . . . from our headquarters!"

"Do you mean that it has nothing to do with you? Can we understand this to be the case?"

"It is of no significance to us. We submit only to orders from our headquarters."

Five o'clock had come and gone. There was nothing unusual in the external appearance of the plane. After consulting with the relief team, I informed Shintani of what had taken place.

Konuma controlled his emotions and listened to Kassay talk about the quantity of fuel, giving his opinions when appropriate. This Kassay was a changed person. No longer did he have the energy of three days ago. The lack of sleep was evident; he kept blinking his eyes. He was no longer steady on his feet when he walked.

Konuma was thinking that it would not be difficult now to get Kassay's gun away from him. There were three others, and since they were also exhausted, the crew members cooperating with each other might be successful in disarming them. But the consequences of failure were evident and fearful. Konuma decided not to make the attempt; he might have had in mind the slogan of the airline, "Be courageous enough to be called a coward."

He asked Kassay where he intended to go.

"Benghazi."

"We might not be able to make it even with full tanks."

"Why not? If the tanks are full, I'm sure we'll make it."

The chief pilot pointed out the potential danger due to the damaged windows, and also that bad weather would make such a long flight impossible.

"We must land somewhere to refuel."

"Maybe that's true," replied Kassay.

"Tell me where you want to land."

"Baghdad?"

"What if landing is refused? If we take off tonight, we'll arrive there in the middle of the night."

Kassay was silent.

"All right. Let's fill up the tanks. The maximum is 260,000 pounds."

Konuma considered the possibility of flying to Athens, where their arrival would be after daybreak. It was probable that landing permission would be refused, but in that event he would make a forced landing. If some other airport permitted landing, that would be all right. His mind was completely made up; he wanted to inform the relief team. There was no way. He knew that there were pilots at the airport, like him, waiting for news.

Professor Shōda also felt that capturing the exhausted Kassay would not be so difficult. He had noticed that one of their number had dozed off almost immediately when he sat down in a nearby seat for a rest. The professor also thought of the great risk involved.

At that time, he had also noticed and memorized the numbers on the grenade in the hijacker's hand, thinking it might be of value later. When, ten minutes later, the man awoke and walked away, he realized he had already forgotten the number. "What a frail thing is human memory," he thought, "in such an extremely tense situation."

At 5:08 Kassay called the tower. "Is the defense minister there? I'd like to speak to him."

"I'm Rashid. What do you want to say?"

"I have a request. Could you refuel the plane?"

"Where to you plan to go?"

No reply.

"I can't give you an answer immediately. Please wait a while."

"All right, but don't take too much time. When the plane is refueled, I'd like to speak to the minister again."

The operations center in Tokyo was strongly against refueling. There was the specter of a crash landing in Israel. They ordered that the plane not be refueled and that negotiations be drawn out.

I could understand the dissatisfaction of newsmen and some members of the relief team. They were saying, "When they demand water or meals, why do you supply them immediately? Why don't you try to have them meet your demands, even gradually? Why don't you bargain with them more?"

I myself was dissatisfied. If we had been in Japan, I would have said, "Do you want meals? If so, release the passengers. If you don't, no food."

Rashid was different. He even proposed supplying water, food, even ice, before they were requested. For our part, we were frustrated by this roundabout approach. Some reporters said, "We're being twisted around the hijackers' little finger. We're continually losing ground."

Finally Kyōno opened our eyes. "It's not a matter of winning or losing. It's the soul of the Arab. . . . Rashid's actions are based on Arab love and compassion, on Arab magnanimity. He desires that those sentiments come alive in the hearts of the terrorists, who are also Arabs."

"The soul of the Arab." It was the first time I had heard those words. I gradually came to appreciate their meaning.

Rashid was trying to make them as comfortable as possible in order to rekindle the "soul of the Arab" and pacify their excited feelings. He was afraid that some slight matter would create displeasure, which in turn could trigger their anger, leading to rashness. He did not want the plane destroyed, and he thought that the way he was taking was the best one to avert this possibility.

After listening to Kyōno's explanation, I realized that the defense minister's way of thinking was little different from mine. It seemed that this would lead to his meeting their demand for fuel. Even so, I did not mind. I thought, "If they want to fly to another airport, I'll fly after them and try to persuade them again to live and let live. I'll go anywhere they go."

But I was the government representative, and my instructions were to settle the matter in Dubai. That, clearly, meant no refueling. I could not ignore the instructions. It was like being in a vice, the government on one side, the terrorists on the other.

At 5:20, "From Mount Carmel to Dubai."

"This is tower. I can hear you well."

"Please call the minister."

"I'm the minister. You want my answer, don't you? Please wait a little longer."

"How long? I can't wait very long. I want the plane refueled as quickly as possible, and then I want to have a talk with you."

"I see. Please wait a little. Then I'll give you my reply."

No one from the relief team heard this. I was at the countermeasures headquarters explaining to about ten reporters the meaning of "soul of the Arab." Just then, a messenger came, saying that the defense minister wanted to speak to Asada and me.

When he saw us he walked rapidly toward us and said, "They're demanding refueling. I'd like to hear the Japanese government's opinion on this matter. Is it yes or no?" His eyes were riveted on us.

We found it difficult to reply. Israel, all hostages killed, ran through my mind. Others had said this was unlikely. But if we refused, there was the possibility that everything would be lost right then and there.

I thought yes was the best answer, but I said, in a loud voice, "No! Our duty comes first," and was instantly shocked by my own words.

Rashid was shocked too, but without hesitation, he picked up the outside telephone and began talking. Kyōno explained that "he seems troubled by the reply of the Japanese side. He's calling his father for advice. From his conversation, it seems he will consult you again."

After ten minutes, Rashid came to us but said nothing. His eyes moved from Asada's face to mine and back again. His face revealed his thought: "Could you reconsider? If not, they blow up the plane."

I nodded my assent to his unasked question, in effect, "Do as you want." He nodded. It was a big gamble on my part.

"Tower, why don't you reply? I want the plane refueled."

"I see. How much do you want?"

"Fill the right tanks first. Then the left ones. On each side, 130,000 pounds."

"It will be done."

"Wait," I said. "There's a condition. Please negotiate for the release of the passengers and half the crew. Tell them that Asada and I will board the plane as hostages. Please put off the refueling until they agree."

"They'll probably refuse," replied Rashid. "I'll tell them after the refueling. But I don't think we can expect agreement."

I said, "Our side is willing to do anything. Tell them to release all the passengers and half the crew–at least the stewardesses."

Preparations for refueling progressed steadily.

From the plane, "Have you completed preparations? We'll tell you when the tanks are full. Anyway, hurry!"

"Preparations will be completed soon. The engineer probably does not speak Arabic. We'll send an interpreter."

"There's no need for that. We'll send one of our comrades down to the ground to supervise."

Asada and I had mixed feelings as we listened to this exchange.

"Why are they stepping up activities so suddenly?" I asked Rashid.

"I'm inclined to believe that there was a key word in the telegram from West Germany. Their movements have become more active since then."

The sender had not been identified. Since the reply had been sent to him and he had received it, he existed, but when the West German police investigated, he had disappeared. (A forty-four-year-old man confessed to sending it, but investigation showed that he was mentally disturbed.) The sender is still unknown.

In the plane tension mounted. The hostages were forced to hold their hands up for an hour; then there was only a ten-minute rest.

Yoshitarō Koga was completely exhausted, his face grimey and sweaty. "What are the government and JAL doing?" he exclaimed.

Others were exhausted. Shigeo Saitō, the president of a company in Tokyo, instead of clasping his hands behind his head, would grasp the back of his seat with both hands. Finally he could not manage even this. When he thought he was not being observed, he would rest his arms by alternately dropping first one and then the other. Once when he was doing this, one of the hijackers passed. Saitō expected a blow on the head with the butt of a pistol, but the man went on without noticing. Perhaps he had taken pity. Saitō was seventy-one. He prayed fervently for the success of negotiations and the release of the passengers.

Shigeharu Hayashi was pale. But his hands were not allowed to come down. Maruoka, apparently taking pity on him, asked, "Are you all right?" Hayashi nodded, and the hijacker said, "Please be patient a little longer," as he rearranged the blanket on Hayashi's knees.

Although Kassay went out of his way to keep Naoko in good spirits, the tension was getting to be too much for her. When he was not talking with the tower, he would come to see how she was getting along. On one occasion, he took her by the hand and led her up to the lounge and into the cockpit, where he allowed her to play. Blankets had been spread on the floor of the lounge and the wreckage hidden. Naoko looked on with curiosity as Kassay talked with the tower.

At 5:44 the message came from the tower, "Preparations for refueling have been completed. We'll send three men. Is it all right?"

"Thank you very much. Tell the men to obey our orders."

"Right. There's a message for you from the Japanese government. Would you like to hear it?"

"No! We receive messages only from . . ."

"Yes. But couldn't you reconsider?"

"No, but we'll study your offer."

Kassay turned to Naoko and, patting her on the head, said, "You're a nice girl. When you grow up, let's you and me fight for the liberation of Palestine."

She stared silently at him, then nodded and said, "Yes." The suggestion had been in Arabic.

Rashid shook his head and said to us, "I tried to relay your message, but it was no use. I'll try again in the name of my government. If they want hostages, we'll provide them. If they want money, we'll give it to them."

"Please do" was all we could find to say.

Arab versus Arab

In Japan it was now 11 o'clock at night. The increased tempo of the hijackers' activity was reported over the telephone circuits, which were still open. At the Ministry of Transport, Shintani was still in his office. At the Pacific Hotel in Shinagawa, members of the passengers' families were demanding to be taken to Dubai. Trying to appease them were Minoru Kimura, JAL's standing director, and Nobuyuki Uchimura, director of the Civil Aviation Bureau.

The defense minister was still at his post in the control tower, as he had been continuously for three days and two nights. He was answering a call from Kassay.

"I'm Rashid. Do you want to speak to me?"

"Yes. Your Excellency, I'd like to give a message to His Excellency the President of the United Arab Emirates. Are you prepared to accept it?"

"Yes, I'm prepared to accept it. Please read it."

"Thank you very much.

"His Excellency the President of the United Arab Emirates:

"In the name of the sons of Palestine, the Sons of Occupied Territory Organizations and the Japanese Red Army faction, I would like to thank you from the bottom of my heart for all the kindnesses you have accorded us and for meeting all of our demands. Your kindness was not unexpected. We were certain that your country would treat us well. That was the reason we chose your country, a pure Arab state, in which to land the plane.

"We are not only grateful for the kindness you have accorded us but also we are very grateful to His Excellency the Defense Minister, who has spent the time together with us since we landed in a friendly country.

"We must apologize deeply for not being able to meet your demands, although you have accommodated all our demands. The reason we cannot meet your demands is that we are commandos and we are soldiers who must obey military orders. We would like to request the defense minister to understand why we cannot act independently.

"We would like to meet you again during the process of the liberation and rehabilitation of Palestine. We would like to request you to fight together with the world's revolutionary forces against international imperialism and Israel.

"May the courageous soldiers who have died for our cause rest in eternal peace!

"May free Palestine and Arab states prosper!

"Group Leader Abbas of the Sons of Occupied Territory Organizations and the Japanese Red Army Faction."

Abbas? This was the first time Kassay had used this name in referring to himself. Here was another man traveling under an alias.

"I have received your message. But I have my duty to perform. I have a request. Will you agree to listen to it?"

"I have given you my message. Now you have a request. I will try to comply if I am able. Also, I have many more requests. I'll probably make them sooner or later. Now I will listen to yours. If I'm able I'll comply immediately."

"In the name of the president and the people of the United Arab Emirates, I, Defense Minister Rashid, request you to release all the men, women and children on the plane. In the name of humanism, I request you to free these innocent people. If that is not possible, I request you to at least release all women and children. Please give me your reply."

"I will. But please wait a little until I prepare it."

Kassay's speech at this stage became a little blurred. He continued, "I'm sorry, but it will be negative. . . . Your Excellency, I have made a sincere Arab pledge that I have not broken. The passengers will never be injured. Before that I'll inflict injury on myself. In injuring myself, I do not mean for the passengers to be injured. I have received clear instructions on the release of the passengers. But I can't release them right now. They will be freed in a short while. I've already promised Your Excellency that I won't harm them. I'd like to repeat that pledge. I won't break it."

"What will become of my honor, the honor of our president and the honor of our people? I've requested you in their names, have I not? You have not taken into consideration all our years of friendly acts toward your brothers in Palestine. I'd like to repeat my request. Please release all women and children. I request this in the spirit and humanity of an Arab, for the honor of Palestine and for ourselves. Please don't become the first one to disgrace our honor."

"Your Excellency, please listen. I do not think of disgracing your honor, or the honor of Dubai and the government of the United Arab Emirates, who have been so kind to us. I've never once thought of disgracing your honor. My honor is part of your honor. We're all Arabs. Our honor is being disgraced by Israel. It is against Israel, which has disgraced our honor, that we are fighting. I can't allow anyone to disgrace our honor.

"As a Palestinian, I have no honor–as an individual or as a citizen. My pride is Jerusalem and Gaza. My pride is Haifa, Jaffa, Saffad. I'm searching for my pride, which has been stolen. I want no one to hurt my pride. It's impossible for me to hurt your pride or disgrace your honor. I respect Your Excellency's pride. The reason I landed in this country is that I knew of its great pride. If this had not been the case, I would have landed in another country. And I would have let no one approach me.

"Your Excellency, do not think that I have any intention of hurting your pride. Your Excellency's words hurt me deeply. Your Excellency has plunged a knife into my heart. I'm a commando. I'm following orders as a soldier."

"No, no! Your pride is my pride. By no means have I hurt you. I'm presently in a very difficult position. I'll allow no one to intervene in what you're trying to do here in an Arab country. My pride does not allow it. Arab problems are my problems. The Palestine problem is the problem of all Arab states."

"Your Excellency! Before bringing this plane to Dubai, I had been to the four corners of the earth. I've had similar experiences in the past. [Perhaps he was referring to the Lufthansa hijack in 1970.] I once went to a country where Arabs were treated most horribly. But thanks to the wisdom natural in Arab countries, I managed to defeat them.

"We are not, like the Europeans, in possession of the weapons of civilization. But we are in possession of pride. I'm in pursuit of pride and I'm fighting for human rights. Is West Germany more humane than us? Has Your Excellency forgotten about Germany in World War I? Or Germany in World War II? What did the Germans do everywhere in the world? What did Hitler do? Why is Willy Brandt helping Israel? Has Your Excellency forgotten the reason he is helping Israel? Has Your Excellency forgotten the Munich [Olympic] massacre? The young men at Munich had no intention of fighting. They only tried to defend themselves. Knowing that Brandt was intent on killing them, they had no alternative but to kill others. In retaliation, we'll teach Brandt a terrible lesson. This is our pride, the pride of all Arab nations.

"As far as I'm concerned, I'll faithfully obey orders from our headquarters. I'm confident I can carry out orders. I have full confidence and trust in our headquarters. They have great confidence and trust in Your Excellency. Therefore, even if I cannot meet your demands, please do not think that relations between Your Excellency and myself will turn bad.

"There is one last request. Your Excellency, could you please hand over the body of Sada, our courageous martyr, to me? She was the one who threw her body over an exploding bomb. Had it not been for her, the plane would have been blown up. I would have died along with all the passengers and crew. Our hero saved the plane and all aboard by sacrificing herself."

"Yes. I'll hand over the body.

"Ever since you came to my country, I have agreed to all your demands in the hope that you would also listen and meet at least some of my own requests. For the release of the passengers, my country and my government are prepared to do anything. We are prepared to pay any amount of money. We are prepared to take any action you may desire."

"Your Excellency, I do not understand what you mean by 'pay.' The message from Japan also mentioned 'money,' but I don't understand at all. Our headquarters, which I absolutely trust, will never place any monetary value on anything it does in the name of the people of Palestine. Of this, I am absolutely sure.

"I have lost a martyr, a soldier, on this plane. That soldier was like the whole world to me. On behalf of this martyr, I'll see that the plane as well as the lives of those on board are protected. However, if I want, the first person I could kill and hand over to you is that guy who was responsible for the death of my comrade Sada [chief purser Miyashita?]. I do not want to kill anyone. I do not want revenge. I will not carry out my revenge on innocent people. And I'm telling the truth. Please believe me. I'll not take out my revenge on any innocent person."

"My fighting comrade! What's your present plan? What do you want to do?"

"Your Excellency! I wanted the plane refueled, and this is being done thanks to your kindness. After that, please hand over the body of my comrade. Then I'd like you to provide me with all information necessary for take-off. I thank Your Excellency from the bottom of my heart. Allah will no doubt bring us together again when Palestine is liberated or on other felicitous occasions."

"Your message is clear. I understand it perfectly.

"I'd like to ask you once more. To you it may seem a very unimportant matter. To me it is of the greatest importance. Please reconsider the release of the passengers and crew. My pride, the pride of my people and of my government are at stake. To protect my pride, I'll offer a compromise. Please free the little girl and her parents. This is the greatest compromise I can make without losing my pride."

"Your Excellency, I'd like to talk to you about the little girl you have just mentioned. In the name of the Arab spirit, the pride of Palestine, my fatherland and all humanity, I make a solemn pledge. She is right now living the happiest and most significant moment of her life. She is now playing beside me. There's nothing special for me to say about the child. I promise that no matter what happens, I'll not be the one to harm her. Please believe me. Do not think that harm will ever come to the child."

"I believe you. I believe in the Arab spirit and Arab humanity. But are you leaving without meeting even one of my requests? Is my demand for the child and her parents so big? My brother! I have great hope in you. Hundreds of reporters are here at this airport. It's impossible for me to believe that you'll take off without considering even one of my requests. My pride, that of my people and of my government are at stake. Can't you please reconsider and free at least the little girl and her parents?"

"Your Excellency, my emotions are running terribly high right now. I'll have to end our conversation. All I can say is that I'll have to wait until I feel calmer–after the plane is refueled–then I'll talk with you again. Please do not call me. I feel terribly confused. Tears stream down my cheeks. I simply cannot continue now."

"I understand how you feel. I'll send the body of the martyr to you. I'll let you know when."

After ten minutes, communication was resumed by Kassay.

"From Mount Carmel to Dubai."

"I can hear you well."

"Your Excellency, from now on, please call this plane as follows: *Jabal Karmel Shahida Sada.*"

He repeated these words four times. They mean "Sada, the Martyr of Mount Carmel."

"I'd like to thank Your Excellency from the bottom of my heart. Please let me know when the corpse is brought to the airport. And please attach to the body the doctor's certificate of death. Treat the body so that it does not emit any foul odor."

"I understand. '*Jabal Karmel Shahida Sada.*' Am I not the first to speak this name?"

The conversation was being interpreted for Asada and myself by Kyōno. I listened in amazement. The men were both Arabs, but there positions were diametrically opposed. They were, in fact, engaged in spiritual talks, as only Arabs could be. It was a thing that I had not imagined would happen.

Although I could report the conversation word for word, space is limited. Moreover, their arguments were woven with great complexity. I would like to mention, however, their sharp exchanges over the interpretation of the Koran. When Rashid would say that Kassay's actions were contrary to the tenets of the Koran, the latter would retort that it was not so, that he was indeed following the Islamic tenets. It occurred to me that only persons brought up in a very religious environment could talk like this.

At this point I would like to take up one question that has not been answered yet: How did the woman known first as Mrs. Peralta and then as Sada die? The doctor who examined the body in Dubai said that "from the way the body was mangled, the explosion must have occurred in the vicinity of her sexual organs. She might have hidden the explosive in her vagina, and it might have exploded unexpectedly." This naturally leads to the question, how could this have happened? Here I must offer what is really a conjecture.

At Schiphol Airport, all the transit passengers were asked to disembark, leaving their hand baggage on the plane. The woman may have felt anxious and wanted to have a weapon with her. Whether this was a hand grenade wrapped in plastic, for example, or some other type of explosive, we do not know.

According to airport records, the passengers were given a simple body check before reboarding. It may be that the woman, afraid of having the weapon discovered, quickly hid it in her vagina. In any case she got through the body check. Her purpose in going to the upper-deck lounge could have been to remove the weapon without being observed. But then the stewardess and, after her, the chief purser went up to the lounge, and the opportunity was lost. It cannot be said with certainty, but the way she was swinging the chair back and forth could have had something to do with setting off the explosive.

There is no doubt that the explosion occurred under her body, and because of this, the fuselage and vital systems were not damaged. But did she sacrifice herself? I think this is most unlikely. I believe the explosion was accidental.

At 6:52 Kassay said, "I was worried that the refueling was being delayed, but it seems that you are doing your best to hurry the operation. I am satisfied. Thank you very much."

"You don't have to worry."

At 7:10 the tower asked, "What are you planning to do about your evening meal?"

"I'll leave it up to you."

At 7:39, "The meals are ready. Are you ready to receive them?"

"Please continue the refueling. We'll accept the meals after that."

At 7:45 Kassay said, "It has become dark. Please put on the lights. Is the coffin ready for the body of the martyr?"

"The coffin has just arrived. It weighs 651 pounds. Please give this information to the chief pilot."

"Okay. I hope there's no odor."

"The body has been expertly treated. We can give you the coffin anytime you desire. Let us know when you are ready."

"I'll do that. Please put on the lights."

"It will be done."

Kassay's language had again started to become rough.

One of the passengers had become ill. Professor Yoshitsugu Kagebayashi of Kinran Junior College (age sixty-two) was suffering from diarrhea. Despite the medicine given him by the stewardess, his condition did not improve. Obviously the long period of tension was having its effect. All the other passengers felt pity, but nothing could be done aboard the plane. Maruoka and Akbal came frequently to see how the professor was getting along.

When Akbal announced that Kagebayashi would be released, there was a great stir among the passengers, but their envious glances soon turned into doubtful glances. Mrs. Kagebayashi, learning that it was only her husband who would be released, burst into tears. She could not believe it. The couple had been touring art museums in Europe; she was almost hysterical at the thought of separation.

At 8:34, "Flight information! Inform us of the temperature, wind velocity and length of the runway."

"Right. We'll have to check the plane. It's been here for three days."

"No! That's absolutely impossible."

By 9:10 refueling had been completed; the tanks were nearly full to capacity (258,000 pounds of the possible 260,000).

"Bring us aviation maps of the Middle East and North Africa. Also a low altitude chart, together with an airport map."

"Right. Tell us why you need a low altitude chart."

"There's no necessity for telling you."

At 9:15 the evening meals were loaded aboard the plane.

"Bring the coffin."

"Do you want to know the size of the coffin."

"Yes."

"It's 8.5 feet long, 2 feet wide and 1.3 feet high."

"Thank you. I'll release one passenger in gratitude for Your Excellency's kindness. This is the most I can do now."

"Who are you releasing?"

"You'll know when he's released. How many men will bring the coffin?"

"Two or three."

"Okay."

"Thank you for your kindness in releasing a passenger."

At 10:25, "We'd like to make our stay here as short as possible. Please hurry with the flight information."

"We'll send all the necessary information."

There was no indication that the defense minister was trying to persuade the hijackers not to leave the airport. Rashid's pride had not been hurt by the promised release of the passenger, but we were furious.

Mrs. Kagebayashi was in a state of hysterics, but no one tried to comfort her. Her husband could do nothing. Just then, Maruoka came and said, "You may also leave, Mrs. Kagebayashi." Her hysterics subsided instantly, and the couple was taken to the first-class compartment.

At 10:56, "We'll release two passengers. Please accommodate them."

"Thank you very much."

"We're waiting for the coffin."

"We'll bring it to you immediately. Before that, we want to ask you one question."

"What do you mean! What's your question? Bring a ramp to the plane quickly. Bring a car for the two. Hurry!"

Walking silently in the moonlight, six soldiers carried the coffin, marching in step. It was loaded aboard the plane and placed in the first-class compartment.

At 11:15, "Thank you. I'd like to thank Dubai for all it has done for us. I will never forget your kindness. I'd like to thank Your Excellency and the people of your country again from the bottom of my heart."

"Yes, I understand."

My feeling of frustration knew no bounds. Only two passengers released and the plane was about ready to take off. I cornered Rashid and said, "Why are you letting them leave? Could you please negotiate once more? Tell them again that Asada and I are ready to give ourselves up as hostages."

Rashid shook his head. "It's probably useless," he said.

I continued to press him. "Please inform them of the Japanese government's proposal. Please let us talk with them."

"They're extremely excited. If we do anything . . . We mustn't excite them further . . ." was his reply.

"I know that's true. I agree with you. But the plane's tanks are full. A Japanese *kamikaze* pilot did not fill his tanks to capacity before taking off on a mission of sure death. Any pilot who filled his tanks to the brim expected to return alive. The hijackers are no longer thinking of dying."

"All right. I'll let you talk with them. But please don't get them any more excited."

At 11:45 Rashid called Kassay. "There's a message from the Japanese government. Will you listen to it?"

No answer.

"Can you hear me?"

"Yes, I can hear you. Read the message."

Rashid stepped away but kept his hand on the microphone switch. His hand was trembling.

I passed a memorandum to Kimura. He grasped the microphone with a shaking hand.

"Hurry and tell him," whispered Rashid. But Kimura, suffering from stage fright, was finding it difficult to speak Arabic. He started mumbling, "From now–Japan . . ."

"Hurry, hurry! Or Kassay will cut off the switch!"

Kimura finally spoke. "I will transmit a message from the government of Japan. Please answer it.

"First release all the passengers and half the crew. Vice Minister of Transport Satō and JAL President Asada are willing to become hostages.

"Second, if you have any monetary demands to make, please do so.

"Third, the pilot of the plane is exhausted. We'd like to send a replacement."

"We refuse all demands."

Kimura could say nothing.

"We can't comply with any requests made by the Japanese government. We can listen only to our own headquarters and the defense minister."

"It's our last request. Can you agree to taking Vice Minister Satō and President Asada as hostages?"

"No. I can listen, but I can't do anything. We're striving to advance the glory of Arab nations. We've united with the Japanese Red Army faction to annihilate imperialism–Japan's and the world's–to fight against American and West German imperialism. We'll continue our fight in the future."

Hearing this, Kimura looked at me and almost shouted, "Mr. Vice Minister, let me make a rebuttal!"

I said, "Go ahead."

Kimura continued, explaining Japan's Middle East policies. He had been at the embassy in Kuwait a long time and was fully informed.

"Japan respects the independence of Palestine. Japan has assisted Palestine economically——"

At this point Rashid abruptly switched off the microphone.

It was 11:50 P.M. when the Kagebayashis were released and, of course, taken straight to a hospital. But the bearded one told the passengers, "The two have been shot outside the plane." As if this were not sufficient, he pointed a gun at his own head and shouted "Bang!"

The passengers were silent. No one was envious.

Rashid made his final call to the plane at 11:55. "I'd like to make one final request. Please take Vice Minister Satō and President Asada aboard and release the child and her parents."

"I've done too much already. I went beyond my authority in releasing the two passengers. I'm sure I'll be punished. But I transcended my authority because I wanted to repay Your Excellency for the kindness you and your people have accorded us. Please understand this."

The plane's engines began to turn over at 11:56.

"I thank the people of this country."

"Please treat the passengers well. It's your responsibility."

"Don't worry."

JA8109 began to taxi two minutes later. The moon was full. It started down the runway at 12:04 A.M., but it seemed to be moving heavily. The plane had been under the desert sun for three days; no maintenance check had been made.

Defense Minister Rashid, still gripping the microphone, suddenly sprang from his chair, shouting, "It's too fast, too fast, too fast!"

President Asada was slumped in a chair, his face in his hands.

I was standing–stiff as a statue.

The plane did not lift off until it reached the end of the runway. It rose slowly. The soldiers in the control tower gave a shout, and those in the shadows of the buildings ran out and clapped their hands in joy.

This considerably annoyed Japanese newsmen, who furiously demanded to know what there was to be happy about. The newsmen remained skeptical when they learned that the soldiers were relieved that the take-off was successful and that there was no ulterior motive.

The entire world was soon informed of the take-off, and in the Arab countries, airport lights were again turned off, the hope being that the JAL plane would pass by. Israel was again plunged into a state of alert. Thinking of Israel, a wave of panic swept through the countermeasures headquarters in Tokyo.

Turning to Rashid, I said, "I'd like to thank Your Excellency for all you have done for us during these three days, on behalf of the Japanese government and the people of Japan. Thank you very much." But my heart was heavy; the incident was not ended. No one could foresee the outcome.

He replied, "We have only done our duty. I'm sorry that we could not solve the incident here. I offer my apologies to the government and people of Japan. I'll advise the airport where the plane lands to do all in its power to ensure the safety of the passengers."

With these gracious words from a man who had kept watch for nearly seventy-two hours, we parted under the control tower.

It was now July 24. Rashid, despite his extreme fatigue, went from there to the hospital to inquire after chief purser Miyashita and Professor and Mrs. Kagebayashi. We ourselves visited the hospital only after dawn had come.

The Flight to Africa

The message received at countermeasures headquarters in Tokyo at 10:40 A.M., July 24, was sent by Susumu Akiyama, second secretary of the Japanese embassy in Damascus.

"The JAL plane landed at Damascus airport at 1:45 A.M. local time (8:45 A.M. Japan time).

"The airport is under the command of the Syrian defense minister and the commander of the air force.

"The Syrians proposed that they provide necessary food and medicine. These were refused.

"The hijackers demanded fuel. The Syrians provided 15,800 pounds. Refueling was completed forty-five minutes ago (3 A.M. local time). It is estimated that the tanks are full, considering that fuel remained after the landing. The hijackers say that they would like to leave Damascus as soon as possible.

"They have ordered the Syrians not to let anyone approach the plane. Airport authorities have complied with this to protect the lives of the passengers."

Akiyama's second report came from the control tower at the airport. "The JAL plane left Damascus at 4:58 A.M. local time (11:58 A.M. Japan time). Destination unknown."

Nineteen minutes after take-off, the plane was again over Beirut. Konuma was flying at a constant altitude of only fourteen thousand feet, because of his apprehension about the damaged windows. Thirty-one minutes from Damascus, the plane passed over Cyprus, and then it was once again over the island of Rhodes.

There a course change of 135 degrees was made, and it began to cut southwest across the Mediterranean. One and one half hours from Rhodes, it was again in desert skies.

The passengers were resigned to their fate, whatever it might be. Before leaving Dubai, they had been ordered to put on life jackets. This was frightening, but strangely enough, after leaving Damascus, the life jackets gave them a feeling of security. They could believe that the terrorists were not planning to kill them, even though they had no idea of where they were being taken, nor of how long their captivity would last.

Motohiko and Fumihiko Furuichi were now seated side by side. Fumihiko, who had been in Algeria for three years, said to his brother, "We're over Africa."

He was quite correct. The plane was circling over Benghazi. Directly below was Baninah Airport.

Kassay, for whom it was the end of a long journey, was requesting permission to land, but the control tower told him to "wait a little."

He became extremely angry.

"Why don't you let us land!" he shouted.

Again the reply was, "Wait a little."

"I can't wait! Tell me whether I can land or not. If the answer is no, I'll blow up the plane."

"We're in consultation. We're not in a position to permit you to land on our own judgment."

"I can understand that. But don't take too long."

Osamu Maruoka was delivering his third lecture. His first had begun, "Our enemy is America . . . Japanese imperialism . . . West Germany . . ." An ideological speech. No one listened.

His second speech was different, and the hostages were attentive. Tears streaming down his cheeks, he said, "The Japanese government did not reply to any of our demands. They said that if we could kill the passengers, then do so. The Japanese government has forsaken you entirely. However, we'll release you all, based on the Arab spirit of love, mercy and magnanimity.

"You must leave the plane within three minutes after it lands. Two minutes after you leave the plane–that is, five minutes after landing–it will be blown up."

This allegation against their own government was completely unexpected and threw the passengers into a state of confusion. They expressed their dissatisfaction in no uncertain terms; some even used obscenities.

Scurrying back and forth, the stewardesses tried to calm the passengers while giving them instructions. "Please throw away all your fountain pens and pencils and anything else with a sharp point. Take off your shoes and tighten your seat belts securely. When deplaning, take the minimum of personal belongings." Some passengers apparently had their minds on other things, for they took from their bags four or five wristwatches and strapped them on their arms. Others thrust jewels into their pockets.

Maruoka was walking amidst the confusion; here and there he was stopped and asked to repeat what he had said. It was perhaps the first time in his life that he had attracted so much attention. He made a third speech, which was a repetition of his second.

It was 6:03 in the morning when the plane landed in Benghazi.

From the exits, the passengers slid down the emergency escape chutes one after the other. The engines were still whining and the plane had not come to a full stop. Some were caught in the blast from the jets and sent tumbling. But they lost no time in increasing the distance between themselves and the plane. As he ran away, Dr. Imura held Naoko tightly in his arms.

Kassay had miscalculated again.

The fuse leading to one of the three stacks of hand grenades burned too quickly. Just as chief pilot Konuma and his crew, Kassay and his cohorts hit the ground, the explosions began. The hijackers, running across the airport, were taken into custody by Libyan police.

The plane began burning from the lounge. Konuma stood stock-still. He later found it difficult to express his feelings at that moment. "As I saw my plane going up in flames, I felt–it was like a sharp knife cutting into my flesh . . ."

The passengers–fortunately all were still alive–were picked up by microbuses and taken to one of the airport buildings. They still did not know where they were.

While everyone's attention was riveted on the plane, Motohiko Furuichi, who had been on the first bus, went in search of airport officials. Approaching a ground hostess, he shouted, "What airline do you belong to?"

It was perhaps a strange question, but she replied, "Libyan Arab Airlines."

"What's the name of this airport?"

"Baninah in Benghazi."

"Could you take me to the man in charge of communications? I'm a staff member of Japan Air Lines." Thus Furuichi was the first to report the Benghazi landing to Tokyo.

At this point, I would like to put in a word about what happened ten minutes after JA8109 left Dubai, though, like so many other things, it remains unexplained. A telegram was received there addressed to the "Sons of Occupied Territory." The sender was "Saurans of Poland" (meaning "Children" of Poland), and the message was "Passengers free. May God be with you."

From the control tower, this message was relayed to Kassay. He sighed with relief.

For my part, I was convinced that the hijackers had changed their minds about dying and that they would eventually free the hostages. I made up my mind to follow the plane and continue negotiations. On my way from a meeting with Prime Minister Rashid Al-Maktoum, I stopped at the airport and learned of the plane's landing.

We wanted to leave right away, but, again, visas were necessary to enter Libya. If we asked the Libyan government to grant them on an emergency basis, I, as a government official, and the relief team could obtain visas, but others, including the newsmen, would find it more difficult. Luckily, the Ministry of Foreign Affairs managed to obtain the Libyan government's agreement to visas for all.

But the foreign ministry also sent instructions that "Ambassador Ishikawa and First Secretary Kimura should return to Kuwait immediately since the incident has been solved."

To say that they were crestfallen is to put it too mildly. They had done all in their power to secure the release of the hostages; they wanted to go to Benghazi. I sympathized with them. Why should they return to Kuwait now? I called Shintani and said, "Ishikawa and Kimura have already boarded my plane. Please understand that the two men will accompany me to Benghazi."

Without waiting for a reply from either Shintani or the foreign ministry, we took off for Athens, where we would have to wait for information from Benghazi. JA8109 was smouldering on the runway; only its tail assembly was intact. Until the wreckage was cleared, it was impossible for another large plane to land.

Although the Libyan government and the state of Benghazi promptly arranged accommodations for them at the Bejira Palace Hotel, the passengers were restless, and some were angry at the airline for being so slow in coming to their rescue. Voices were heard exclaiming:

"What's JAL doing? What bad service!"

"Hey stewardess, being me some coffee!"

"Isn't there any Japanese tea? What bad service!"

Before the plane had been destroyed, the passengers, for the most part, had behaved as meekly as lambs, patiently waiting for the time when they would be free. Now that they were, they were giving vent to emotions that they had been forced to keep in check for eighty-two hours. They looked for scapegoats, and the ones closest at hand were those, particularly the stewardesses, who were wearing the uniform of Japan Air Lines.

It is immediately apparent that the stewardesses were every bit as much victims as the passengers; in fact they had suffered greater mental strain, for they had been caught between their duty of looking after the passengers and the necessity of trying to assuage the excitable guerrillas. Physically and mentally, the stewardesses were the more exhausted, but some people did not take this into consideration.

There was no Japanese tea in Libya. Although not openly, some stewardesses broke down and wept at these outrageous demands, and there were among the passengers those who tried to comfort them. This, however, led to the sympathizers being pounced on by what we may now call the "angry group."

Next, it was the Japanese government that came in for criticism. Maruoka's words were still fresh in their minds, and that had been their only information during the long period of confinement. They actually believed him and criticized their own government in no uncertain language. Aggravating the situation was the delay in the arrival of the relief team.

We were still in Athens waiting for conditions to allow us to land at Baninah, but as an alternative we were also requesting permission to fly to Tripoli. Neither permission was immediately forthcoming, so we had to reschedule our departure from Athens for the next day (July 25). Asada was in contact with his staff in Benghazi, and when he learned of the passengers' behavior, he advised them, "I can understand their behavior. I'll apologize later for the sufferings they have gone through. But tell the crew to take good care of them. I know how tired they are." He felt a sense of guilt in that he had not been able to effect the rescue personally.

It was not that the recently released hostages were not being taken care of. Through the courtesy of the government, the Libyans had, among other things, piled a table in the hotel high with underwear and shirts and pants, with the intention that each passenger should receive one set. However, by the time the latecomers arrived, there was nothing left for them. At first, the JAL staff thought that things had been miscounted, but the soldiers who had brought the clothing assured them that everything had been counted twice.

When this happened a second time, the passengers themselves were sharply critical, but none of the early comers came forth with their hastily acquired extra ration.

Another incident centered around a bus provided, also by the government, for a sightseeing trip through Benghazi. When it arrived at the hotel, the first reaction from the "angry group" was that they had not "come here for sightseeing," and only a few boarded the bus. After the JAL staff announced that money spent on shopping in the city would be reimbursed by the airline, the bus was full in no time at all. Then those who could not get on complained, saying that the airline should provide a second bus.

Those who went returned to the hotel without having purchased anything, because the shops throughout the city were closed. Not content with attributing this to bad luck, some began to insinuate that JAL had known all along that this was the case. It should be pointed out that most of the passengers did not agree with this interpretation.

The reader may be wondering about the behavior of the "angry group." Why, it may be asked, did not the passengers fall into two groups: those who were in a state of shock and unable to do anything but go along with the situation, and those whose elation at being alive and free was so great that inconveniences in their present situation could be overlooked? It is a difficult question, the answer to which, I believe, can only be found in an understanding of Japanese psychology.

While they were captive, the passengers were not in a rational state of mind that would permit them to understand their position and wait for rescue. The terrorists' guns kept them quiet, but in their hearts were anger and dissatisfaction, and their emotions could erupt suddenly. They were obsessed with what is called *higaisha ishiki*, or "victim consciousness." Psychologists regard this as a changed form of *amae*. (*Amae*, which may be translated as "dependence" or "indulgence," is a concept important to the understanding of Japanese psychology. Space does not, however, permit a discussion here; Professor Takeo Doi of the University of Tokyo discusses it at length in *The Anatomy of Dependence* [Tokyo: Kodansha International, 1973].)

In Japan, it is not rare for drivers who have caused death or injury to commit suicide because of excessive demands made on them by the injured, or survivors in the case of death. In the present instance, as I have mentioned, members of the passengers' families were very demanding toward both the airline and the government. After returning to Japan, I learned that one man, unappeased by the explanations made by the minister of transport, insisted that the prime minister himself do the explaining.

The nature of the offense (airline crash, industrial pollution or whatever) is not the critical factor. Scholars of psychology analyze the phenomenon in terms of the victim's desire to bring the offender down to the same level at which he finds himself. Consequently, he will first direct his attack against a person who is in a relatively weak position. If that person is brought down to his level, he will then turn his attention to another who is in a relatively weak position. Since neither his actions nor his demands are rational, he may make demands on a person who is completely unable to meet them. The behavior is, in a sense, analogous to that of a spoiled child.

That their anger should have been directed against the hijackers is obvious, but with the latter's surrender to Libyan authorities, the only "offender" left was the airline. It stands to reason that not only the passengers and the crew of the plane had been victims but the airline itself. A majority of the passengers understood it in this way, but there was still the "angry group." (It may not be inappropriate to point out that the cost of the jumbo jet, now unsalvageable, when it had been purchased only sixteen months earlier was approximately 25 million dollars.)

Other events reflected a different spirit, and I would also like to tell about those. After the distribution of the relief goods, there was a group who had received none. They were in the reception room of the hotel, where empty cartons that had contained the clothing lay scattered about. A soldier who had helped bring the goods began to tidy up, and the Japanese spontaneously began to help him and continued until the room was again tidy. This led the man to mutter to himself that "the Japanese are kind people." It seems that in Libya unless a man is requested to do so, he will not volunteer to help another.

To be sure, the "angry group" had provoked a reaction. No one knows who did it, but on the wall of the reception room, a notice had appeared, written in Japanese: "To the Passengers: The relief goods have been supplied through the courtesy of the Libyan government. Let us accept them with dignity befitting the people of Japan."

That evening when soldiers brought travel kits, containing toothbrushes, shampoo, lotions and razors, each passenger received one.

With the relief plane still in Athens, JAL staff members were at a disadvantage, at least as far as material comforts were concerned (there was no JAL office in Libya), but others were coming to the rescue. Driving through the desert from Tripoli was Mitsuaki Fukuda, an employee of C. Itoh and Company. He had collected all the rice he could get his hands on and had prepared *nigirimeshi* (rice balls) for two hundred people. Into the large Benz he was driving, he had also loaded other Japanese foods, such as *tsukudani* (fish, vegetables or meat preserved by boiling down with soy sauce) and *fukujinzuke* (vegetables sliced and pickled in soy sauce). With him were Seiichi Narita, of Mitsubishi Trading Company, Takeshi Kambara, of Nissho-Iwai, another trading company, and Jutarō Tsuchida, a special correspondent of the *Asahi Shimbun*, who was stationed in Geneva. The drive, two hundred miles longer than the air distance because of having to go around the Bay of Sidra, took them twelve hours.

When Kōichi Saitō learned of the landing at Baninah, he rented a truck, loaded instant noodles, instant coffee and canned foods on it and departed for Benghazi. He managed to cover the distance in ten hours. He was the manager of Marubeni Trading Company's Tripoli office, and he took with him his staff–Hajime Ueno, Tetsuo Masuno, Kazutō Kihara and Hoshito Kameyama–as well as Masohiro Asano, who had recently come from the head office. Faces grimey and covered with dust, they arrived looking more like men of the desert than what they actually were.

Nearer at hand were Nishimura and Yamagata, who were engaged in the construction of a microwave station near Benghazi. They had been taking care of the passengers since the landing.

As they had done on the Arabian Peninsula, the trading companies, normally rivals, were cooperating in the volunteer relief work.

The relief plane took off from Athens a few minutes after noon on July 25, and a few minutes later a second JAL DC8 left Orly Airport in Paris with nine flight crew and one mechanic. It was necessary to fly to Tripoli and there charter two Friendships for the flight to Benghazi.

President Asada was downcast. I could understand how he felt. "It's a question of what attitude you should take," I said. "It's because they're alive that the passengers are angry. It's only because of that that they can feel anger, cry, laugh or express any other emotion. Yes, only because they're alive! Let's listen patiently to everything they have to say.

"I've made a *waka*, like this: 'You, passengers/Pray, dance, be happy/Speak to your heart's content/Morning in Benghazi!'

"Let's listen to what they have to say, for three hours, or even five hours."

Breaking into a smile, he replied, "Yes, Mr. Vice Minister, let's do that. I'll listen to whatever complaints they have."

At the Bejira Palace Hotel, as they waited, most of the passengers spent the time resting in their rooms, but those with complaints took to roving through the hotel, searching for scapegoats. They did not even look tired.

"Why is the arrival of the relief plane so late?"

"What's the Japanese government doing?"

"JAL's service is bad!"

"The food we're getting here is poor."

Aside from their fellow passengers, they were not particular about which of their fellow countrymen they made their grievances known to. The trading company employees who had come to their assistance were not spared. When one of the men who had crossed the desert from Tripoli replied to a question by saying that he did not know when the relief plane would arrive, this brought down a shower of complaints. He would have liked to point out that he was not an employee of the airline but felt that this might embarrass his questioners, and he did not want to do that. But he continued with his work anyway.

Realizing that man's needs go beyond clothing, the Benghazi municipal government hit on the idea of letting its guests pass the time in swimming–and promptly provided swimsuits.

In the matter of communication, it was once again a trading company that provided the only fast, direct link. Messages from Benghazi were sent to Tripoli and thence via Marubeni's telex to its head office in Tokyo.

The two relief planes landed in Tripoli within three-quarters of an hour of each other. It was impossible for the DC8s to go on to Baninah, for although the airport could normally accept a jumbo jet, less than one mile of runway was usable. We chartered two Friendships and left Tripoli at 5:05 A.M., arriving in Benghazi at 7:02. Waiting for us were the governor of the state of Benghazi and the mayor of the city.

The Bejira Palace Hotel, which is not unlike a European hotel, has seen its bit of history. Benito Mussolini had stayed here on an inspection tour of the African front during World War II. And in the desert not far away, Field Marshal Rommel had led the combined German and Italian forces in a fierce battle with British tanks. The color of the desert was red, like blood and rusting iron. I composed a *waka*: "They live still/though stung by the *gamul*/ The plane went up in flames/at Baninah." (*Gamul* is a thorny plant.)

Tumbling down the emergency chutes and scrambling to get clear of the plane–through the thorny *gamul*–few of the passengers had escaped being scratched and receiving minor injuries. Their bandaged arms and legs were not a pleasant sight. I found that I did not have words enough to comfort them.

But their eyes–some were still angry at the length of time it had taken for us to arrive. "What's the government . . .?" For the moment, I kept silent, but then both Asada and I tried to explain what had happened. I began by saying, "I'm overwhelmed by joy to be able to meet you here. I have no words to express my pleasure at being able to see you alive."

I then went on to apprise them of all that had happened: how I had learned of the incident, the establishment of the countermeasures headquarters, my selection as the government's representative, the departure of the relief team, the intention of solving the incident in Dubai, Sheikh Rashid's wholehearted efforts, the absence of demands, the government's willingness to make concessions, the offer of alternate hostages, the threats to blow up the plane, and ended by saying, "When I saw the plane take off from Dubai, the only thing I could do was to pray for your safety. We flew over Benghazi a little past noon today. From the control tower we heard that you were relaxing. We were quite relieved.

"Two relief planes are waiting for you in Tripoli right now. The president has ordered the wreckage here to be cleared away in one day, but the reopening of Baninah will take two or three days. I'm grateful to the Libyan government and would like to wait here with you until it is reopened. Please feel free to say anything. Together with Mr. Asada and Ambassador Ishikawa, I'll try to solve any problems you may have."

Asada began his explanation by saying, "For the past three days I've been thinking about your safety, and I'm afraid I haven't had much sleep. Please excuse me if my memory is a little faulty."

He then went on to mention, among other things, his attempts to talk with Maruoka and the negative reply that had received, and ended by saying, "Now, my fervent wish is to get you back to Tokyo as quickly as possible, where members of your families are waiting. The airport is expected to be usuable in the morning, although I do not know the exact time. When it is, I'll make arrangements for the two planes to come from Tripoli and pick you up. I promise to return you to Japan as fast as possible."

Then, for three whole hours, we were kept busy answering questions. But "questions" is not quite the right word; it was more like listening to complaints. What particularly irritated the passengers was the alleged delay in rescue work and Maruoka's inflammatory statement about the government. Between the passengers there were also verbal exchanges, one man, for example, saying that the hijacking had delayed his return to Japan and thus endangered the successful completion of the business he had been conducting in Europe, and someone else wanting to know if the return of a businessman should take precedence over the return of a tourist who had been saving all his life for the trip. There was even disagreement (from women) when someone expressed his intention of offering thanks for the splendid job the JAL staff had done.

Eventually, though, everyone said what he had on his mind, and we all retired.

The next morning finally brought forth bright and cheerful faces, so I was able to breathe a sigh of relief. And I felt like composing a *waka*: "While eating watermelon/I reminisce over Rommel/Morning has come to Benghazi."

The first plane left Baninah that afternoon (July 26) at 1:13, carrying all but one of the Japanese passengers and some of the relief team, including President Asada. My own departure, with the non-Japanese passengers and the rest of the relief team, was delayed by a malfunctioning fire extinguisher in the number three engine, for which replacement parts had to be brought from Cairo. We left a little after 10 that night.

The members of my staff who were with me, and also those in Tokyo, were rather disappointed by this. They had, of course, worked very hard with me during my election campaigns and were well aware that my getting off the first plane in the glare of television cameras would be great publicity for my next campaign. This was not to be. As the government representative, my duty was to return only after all others had been taken care of.

Professor Shōda, who had stood aside from the heated discussion of the previous evening, also volunteered to wait for the second plane. When we landed at Schiphol Airport, it was the early hours of July 27. One week had passed.

In Amsterdam I was informed that chief purser Miyashita and Professor and Mrs. Kagebayashi were on their way home and would arrive before our plane did.

Of the five non-Japanese passengers, only one reboarded the plane in Amsterdam. He was a Swiss by the name of Hans Mueller, who was employed by a trading firm in Paris. Not only had his family and many of his friends come to the airport but Swiss newspapers had carried pictures and banner headlines announcing his safe return. He carried a bunch of the newspapers as he took his seat.

"Why didn't you get off here?" I asked.

He replied, "I didn't want to discontinue my trip. My family and friends tried to persuade me to do so, but I'm going on to Japan. It's my job to go and purchase ships. It's my duty to see that my job is completed."

To me his reply was quite clear. I could understand a man who felt that he had to be faithful to his duty.

July 27, 4:43 A.M.: The first relief plane arrived at Tokyo International Airport. Minister of Transport Shintani shook hands with each passenger as he got off the plane.

At 10:35 P.M. the plane carrying the Kagebayashis arrived. They were greeted by Shintani and Asada and chose to remain at the airport until the arrival of the second plane.

July 28, 3:35 A.M.: We arrived in Tokyo. While the others

disembarked, I went to the cockpit and thanked the chief pilot, copilot and flight engineer for bringing us home safely. I was the last one to get off the plane.

The airport was silent–no crowds, no television cameras. I caught sight of Shintani standing at the foot of the ramp and waving to me.

"I didn't have time to spend the two hundred thousand yen he gave me as a farewell gift," I muttered.

Epilogue

Four months after the Dubai incident, there was a cabinet reshuffle. There was nothing unusual in this; under Japan's parliamentary system, cabinet reshuffles are not uncommon and can and do occur at various times, whether or not there have been recent elections. Minister of Transport Shintani submitted his resignation on November 24, 1973.

What was unusual was that when I offered my resignation to the new Minister of Transport, Masatoshi Tokunaga, two days later, it was not accepted. There had been another hijacking.

At 2:55 A.M. that day, Palestinian guerrillas had hijacked a KLM plane over Baghdad. Although there were no Japanese among the terrorists this time, there were Japanese among the 170 passengers, and the government decided to establish a countermeasures headquarters. Thus was my resignation postponed.

I cabled Defense Minister Rashid to enlist his assistance, and he replied, "I received your cable regarding the KLM incident. If the plane lands in the United Arab Emirates, I'll do all I can to protect the lives of the passengers and crew just as I did in the JAL hijack. Our action in that case was based on humanitarianism. I am confident that Allah will solve everything peacefully and that evil will be destroyed."

The demands of the hijackers were the closing of a camp for Jewish refugees in the Netherlands and the release of seven Palestinian guerrillas imprisoned in Cyprus. These demands were met and the passengers and crew were released, but it took two days.

That no demand was made for the release of the four JAL hijackers, still under detention in Libya, is indicative of the complicated structure of the guerrilla organizations.

January, 1974, found me again in Dubai, as the leader of a small group of fellow members of the Diet belonging to the Liberal Democratic Party's Middle East Economic Cooperation Team. The Yom Kippur war had taken place, the OPEC had imposed its oil embargo, and it was time for Japan to reassess its policies toward the Arab states. It might be said that there was an "Arab boom" in Japan at that time.

Half a year before that, Sheikh Rashid had remarked, "Our country has practically nothing to offer you. But the moon shining emerald green over the desert and the stars are the most beautiful in any Arab country. I'd like you to view our moon and stars someday." Naturally I had promised to return, and the moon and stars were indeed beautiful.

One of my objectives during that trip was to obtain information on Fusako Shigenobu. I was able to make contact with a number of Arabs who were well informed about the guerrilla organizations, and they advised me that "when she came from Japan, she was welcomed warmly. And when her husband (Junzō Okudaira) and Kōzō Okamoto and another man carried out the massacre at Lod Airport, they went wild with joy. But when Maruoka and the others hijacked the JAL plane and demanded a huge amount of ransom money, the guerrillas began to turn a cold shoulder on Shigenobu and her Japanese comrades, saying, 'We're not bandits. We have our pride as Arabs.' Because of the fear of adverse world opinion, the guerrillas are not in favor of hijacking aircraft on which there is a large number of innocent passengers. Today, among the Palestinian guerrilla organizations, Shigenobu and her cohorts are evidently outcasts."

At that time, Kassay (or Abbas), Maruoka, the man who called himself Peralta and Akbal were on trial before a court in Benghazi. The Libyan government was reported to be taking a severe attitude toward them, regarding them not as political prisoners but as common criminals. The court announced that it would pass sentence according to Islamic law, which could mean that they would have their arms cut off. But there were other opinions, sympathetic to the prisoners, which said in effect that they were mere soldiers, excellent soldiers who faithfully obeyed orders. It is my belief that such sympathetic opinions reflected the bad reputation of the guerrilla organizations.

Around the end of January, when I returned from my trip, two Arabs and two Japanese attacked an oil storage complex in Singapore. When this proved unsuccessful, they hijacked a ferry and kept it offshore. At this juncture, I conferred with Ambassador Tōkichirō Uemoto in Singapore by telephone and advised him of the approach taken by Rashid, but the incident expanded with the occupation by guerrillas of the Japanese embassy in Kuwait and the taking as hostages of Ambassador Ishikawa and First Secretary Kimura.

Demands were made for the transportation of the four involved in the Singapore incident to Kuwait, where they joined the others, and for a JAL plane to be flown to Kuwait–with twenty JAL pilots, who also became hostages. This incident was mediated by the PLO, and the hostages were released safely.

In the middle of the summer of 1974, Osamu Fukunaga, a friend about whom I shall have more to say shortly, returned from Europe with the following report: "While in prison, Kōzō Okamoto seems to have changed his ideology. Maruoka and the other three are still in prison and will no doubt be tried as criminals, but there seems to be a rapprochement between the Libyan government and the PLO, so there is a possibility that the trial will be only a formality before the hijackers are handed over to the PLO as political prisoners. Shigenobu has not been informed of this."

I could not understand why the four, who had caused such misery and anguish to the passengers, should be allowed to get off lightly, but that is exactly what happened.

Before they were released, however, another incident occurred. Information filtered in from Europe that guerrillas would occupy a Japanese embassy in Europe with the objective of having the JAL hijackers released. Then in July, 1974, Paris police arrested Yoshiaki Yamada, alias Suzuki, for illegal entry. The passport he carried was counterfeit, and he also had in his possession an order presumably written by Shigenobu. On the basis of his confession, the French authorities arrested and deported several Japanese.

The attack came on September 13 in The Hague, but the embassy was French rather than Japanese. Ambassador Jacques Senard and ten members of the embassy staff were taken hostage. And this time there was violence. The guerrillas opened fire on Dutch police, seriously injuring one male and one female police officers.

The attackers, three Japanese youths, demanded that "Suzuki" be released, that a plane be put at their disposal, and that ransom be paid in the amount of three hundred thousand dollars. After five days, the Dutch and French governments acceded to these demands, and an Air France Boeing 707 flew the terrorists from Schiphol to Aden. The government of the People's Democratic Republic of Yemen permitted landing and refueling but not disembarkation. From there the plane was flown to Damascus, and the guerrillas gave themselves up to Syrian authorities.

Arab countries are very kind to their guests. It is a characteristic of the people. From this point of view, I do not think that Shigenobu and other Japanese (some say fifty, others say one hundred) who are in Arab countries are being treated badly. Still, the PLO did not mediate in the attack on the French embassy, nor did the government of Yemen, which had been sympathetic to the guerrillas, permit the terrorists to stay in that country. And the Syrian authorities not only arrested them but confiscated the ransom money and their weapons.

Although Shigenobu and the others are not being treated badly by their hosts, it is becoming clear that they are unwelcome guests.

When our plane stopped in Anchorage on the way back to Tokyo, I purchased a number of fountain pens and ballpoint pens. These I inscribed "Dubai——Benghazi/0——100 rescue operation/B. Satō 21.7.1973." These I wanted to give to all the persons who had assisted me in the rescue operation.

Zero or one hundred . . . There was nothing in between. If even one of the passengers had been killed, the rescue operation would have been a failure. It can be imagined how happy I felt as we flew back to Tokyo secure in the knowledge that the rescue operation had been 100 percent successful.

I would like to express my deepest gratitude to Sheikh Muhammad ibn Rashid Al-Maktoum and to all the others who gave their unwavering cooperation and assistance.

In Libya, I had watched the sun set. When the evening glow was at its most beautiful, my heart was full of emotion. In the splendor of the crimson sun, I had seen a figure, the figure of a man. I made a sketch in my notebook, and after I returned, I made an oil painting, which was included in an exhibition of works done by men in the political and business worlds. (The exhibition was sponsored by the Diet League for the Promotion of the Arts.)

This figure of a man, which might be described as a he-man, I saw again. At the time I was writing this epilogue, the scene on the television screen was of the French embassy in The Hague. Even as a pistol was being pointed at his back, Ambassador Senard smiled. And later at Schiphol, the Dutch pilot of the Air France plane rolled up his sleeves and nonchalantly climbed aboard. Here were two more men . . .

After World War II, I met in the bombed-out rubble of the city of Oita a man named Osamu Fukunaga, and then ten years later I met him again at Oita Station. He was a newspaper reporter then, and he was on his way to cover the Sugo Incident, which involved public security in Oita Prefecture. His coverage earned him the first Japan Journalists' Congress Prize.

After another period of ten years, our paths crossed again at Hakata Station in northern Kyushu. He was then a magazine reporter headed for the port of Sasebo, where the USS *Enterprise* was soon to dock. Students were demonstrating against the entry of the aircraft carrier, and my path lay in the same direction, for I was then chairman of the Liberal Democratic Party's Student Countermeasures Committee. We met many times after that: during the dispute over the construction of Narita airport, during the Red Army incident, in fact, whenever there was an incident, we seemed to meet.

This book was made possible by the assistance of Fukunaga and many other friends. I would like to express my gratitude particularly to Stanley R. Rader and Professor Osamu Gotoh of Ambassador College, Los Angeles; Teikichi Tarusawa of Kodansha Ltd.; and Yukimori Akanoma, Tokio Uetsuhara and Homer Neal of Kodansha International.